Salted With Fire

TO STEPH
MAY WE All CONTINUE
TO GROW IN THE
GRACE AND KNOWIEDGE
OF CHRIST

Salted With Fire

A Gift for the Body of Christ

John Van Tuyl

To order additional copies of this book, contact:
Xlibris Corporation
1-888-795-4274
www.Xlibris.com
Orders@Xlibris.com
45166

Contents

Preface

Salted With Fire—A Gift for the Body of Christ is a challenging exposé into the purposes of God through His fiery dealings with mankind. *Salted With Fire* offers some fresh insights into such things as the mystery of the "second death." It explores the difference between the *spirit* and the *soul* and how every man's encounter with our Father's all-consuming nature (fire) shall ultimately come to be understood as the greatest of blessings.

This book has been written with the spiritually hungry person in mind. The maturing soul is instinctively craving a well-balanced meal. Yet, the only indication a person may experience is a discovery they are no longer satisfied by the milk and pabulum commonly served as Sunday fare.

Understanding the relationship of our spirit, soul and body to God's ultimate purpose is a topic of almost universal appeal. *Salted With Fire* is an in-depth look into the makeup of man. Also revealed is the dynamic involvement of our Father to conform humanity onto the image of His Son.

Salted With Fire challenges many dead-end religious paradigms. These mindsets are steeped in the traditions of men and tend to keep God's people spiritually crippled in infancy. Those who venture to read this book should be prepared to entertain some fresh perspectives. In due course, the patient reader will find that these pages extend a message of hope and great confidence in Christ. Overall, it is a message that offers help for those who struggle to stay afloat in a tempest-tossed sea of post-modern thought.

The core issue this book addresses is the transformation of the soul. Because such varied understandings exist, and some confusion as to the nature of the soul, I am wont to define this: Our living *soul* is merely the temporal experience of our *mind, will, and emotions* with an indelible memory of that experience that persists after shedding this mortal coil.

To help facilitate a deeper understanding, this book draws a clear distinction between our *soul* and the *being* we are spiritually. This distinction leads to a head-on confrontation with the illusion we have come to accept as ourselves—the mind-manufactured self, the ego. It would seem that somehow we have come to think of ourselves as the sum total of our thoughts. Oops!

By chipping away the accumulation of centuries of religious thinking, the true beauties of God's jewels are then revealed. The removal of this accretion may well seem to be unprecedented or trailblazing. Yet in truth, one has only rediscovered what was from the beginning.

While *Salted With Fire* is addressed primarily to the Body of Christ, it is written in such a way that any person may find it interesting. Even those who may have rejected Christianity (based on the hypocrisy they have witnessed) will find the message contained in these few pages a life changing experience.

The author has not written as a scholar might write, claiming to be some authority, or having the last word on any subject. Rather, it is written by one who bears a profound message of transformation. Indeed, this powerful message has so impacted the author's life that in many respects he has become the message.

May its impact continue to abound onto the Glory of God and greater good of all!

Sincerely

John Van Tuyl

"He answered and hath said, `Lo, I am seeing four men loose, walking in the midst of the fire, and they have no hurt; and the appearance of the fourth is like to a son of the gods.'"

Daniel 3:25

Young's Literal

Introduction

Jesus plainly said,

> For *everyone* will be *salted with fire,* and *every sacrifice* will be *salted with salt.* (Mark 9:49; italics mine)

Parabolic translation:
For *everyone* will be *purified,* and *every sacrifice* will be *preserved.*

That may seem an extremely bold statement. However, it only garners its boldness from the fact that it flies in the face of commonly accepted dogma. To some degree, the rhetoric of Evangelical Churchianity has distorted our hearing.

Can it be possible that our Omnipotent God and Loving Father all along had a plan to accomplish this cleansing? Is this extraordinary statement, as some would attest, merely a "wishful thought" on our Savior's part? It is my contention that this is not by any means "wishful thinking." Mankind's Father has a plan that covers every contingency of the human condition. His marvelous plan is so perfect it even transcends our apparent lack to understand or appreciate it. Additionally I contend, due to the incredible dullness of man's perception, that our Father's plan has remained hidden when all the while it was being displayed openly in plain sight.

Nevertheless, Jesus testifies to us:

> For nothing is hidden that will not become evident, nor anything secret that will not be known and come to light. So take care how you listen; for whoever has, to him more shall be given; and whoever does not have, even what he thinks he has shall be taken away from him. (Luke 8:17-18)

I hear the Spirit saying,

Pay very close attention to how you listen. Because only to the one whose understanding proves to be founded in truth shall even greater understanding be given. To the one whose understanding proves false, or to be a misunderstanding, even what he was so sure he possessed will dissolve in the light of Truth—in other words, *be taken away from him.*

11

The intention of the book you now hold in your hand is to test our understanding beyond its breaking point. Thanks be unto God, our Father's Truth transcends the realm of opinion. In other words, if something is actually true, it cannot be broken. Only illusions have fault lines where they may be broken.

If men will be diligent in "how they hear," the Spirit of God will see to it that their understanding is fully pruned of any deadwood of falsehood or misunderstanding. For the Holy Spirit has been given the responsibility and specific commission of leading us into all truth.

> As for you, the anointing which you received from Him abides in you, and you have no need for anyone to teach you; but as His anointing teaches you about all things, and is true and is not a lie, and just as it has taught you, you abide in Him. (1 John 2:27)

If we will only take our Father at His Word, no longer will we find ourselves desperate to hold the brittle pieces of our understanding together, rather, we shall now find our understanding happily holding us.

By acquiring an unbreakable understanding directly from our Father, we shall find the trustworthy branches of the Tree of Life effortlessly upholding us. In truth, this is that peaceful state of untroubled rest for which every heart hungers.

I suggest that you do not read this book per se, but rather that you would meditate your way through it. Only what the Spirit is saying to you personally is of any paramount importance. As you feel these words apply pressure on your understanding, take them as merely directing your attention to listen to God's Spirit. Allow the pressure. If your understanding is actually trustworthy, rest assured it will not break.

Again, *how* we hear is far more important than *what* we hear! Because in listening to *God's* holy anointing, it exposes not only the veracity of whatever we hear but also the validity of our current understanding.

By His guidance, "perfect love casts out all fear." If you come away from this experience with nothing more than a revelation about a "hearing ear," I shall rest in the surety of your ultimate freedom!

Following three years of an intense walk with His disciples, Jesus said, "You are already clean because of the word which I have spoken to you." For more than three years, Jesus had been breaking off every lifeless religious branch encumbering their understanding.

However, during this period of instruction, the disciples seldom understood the words of Jesus; yet nonetheless, they had become the unwitting recipients of profound truths. Not one of them was truly aware of what they had received until the day of Pentecost. It was then that the illuminating fire of God brought back to remembrance all the Truth Jesus had invested in them. With that said, let us now launch into the deep and explore the miracle-working *fire* of God.

Initially, we have this familiar testimony from John the Baptist:

> I indeed baptize you in water to repentance; but He who is coming after me is stronger than me, of whom I am not able to lift the sandals. He will baptize you in the *Holy Spirit* and *Fire*, whose fan is in His hand, and He will cleanse His floor and will gather His wheat into the storehouse. But He will burn up the chaff with unquenchable fire. (Matthew 3:11-12; italics mine)

If these verses are read with what would be called a traditional religious mind-set, we shall easily find ourselves slipping into an *us-versus-them* mentality. This rigidly calcified mind-set is one we never find Jesus advocating. After all, it was our Lord's cavorting with the unwashed masses that so incensed the sanctimonious Pharisees!

Therefore, for the purpose of our exploratory study in fire, we will try to keep our attention confined to our Father's dealings with the wheat and the chaff within the intricacy of our own soul.

All throughout the growing season, the hard outer shell of the husk has served a vital life-sustaining purpose by protecting the maturing wheat. However, at harvest time, it no longer serves a useful purpose. At this time, the useless chaff is removed from the valuable wheat.

Please take note that in the preceding verse, the word *unquenchable* does not, in any way, imply anything approaching the meaning of the word *eternal*. It merely denotes the nature of God's fire as being beyond any man's ability to extinguish.

Everyone's baptism in Holy Fire shall burn until it has accomplished the purpose for which it was intended, namely the total consumption, or the complete destruction, of every *unregenerate aspect* of the first creation.

Only through God's destruction of the outer chaff is the wheat of the new creation unveiled. When our Father reveals His glory in the perfect workmanship of His new-creation man, it shall mean the entire transfiguration of His corporate Son. "And every eye shall see Him!"

> When He comes to be glorified in His saints on that day, and to be marveled at among all who have believed. (2 Thessalonians 1:10)

Marveled at? No doubt that when bathed in the awesome light of His Majesty, many shall be rendered speechless! However, at this particular time, *our Lord will be glorified only in those saints who have overcome this world's influence, their fleshly nature, and the spirit of deception.*

It would be safe to say that our brother, the apostle Paul, was a believer. Yet it seems Paul had caught a glimpse of something even greater, a pearl of unspeakable value and worth! Throughout his ministry, Paul's passion for this *prize* would become his primary reason for drawing breath in the face of great suffering. The acquisition of this pearl would overshadow Paul's focus and would energize all his labors of love!

Paul writes,

> In order that I may attain to the resurrection from the dead [the first resurrection]. *Not that I have already obtained it* or have already become perfect [as a fully mature Son], but I press on *so that I may lay hold* of that for which also I was laid hold of by Christ Jesus. Brethren, *I do not regard myself as having laid hold of it yet*; but one thing I do: forgetting what lies behind and reaching forward to what lies ahead, *I press on toward the goal for the prize of the upward call of God in Christ Jesus.* (Philippians 3:11-14; italics mine)

Clearly, Paul's vision of this hard, sought-after *prize* greatly exceeded rejoicing in his imagined ticket to "Gloryland."

May I, at this time, gently remind us of the many cautionary statements that have been lovingly made to all believers:

14

I advise you to buy from me gold [divine nature] refined by fire so that you may become rich, and white garments so that you may clothe yourself [with the mind of Christ], and that the shame of your nakedness [Adamic nature] will not be revealed and eye salve to anoint your [mind's] eyes so that you may see [beyond mere appearances]. (Revelation 3:18)

Let all who have ears give heed to what the Spirit is saying to the churches. He who overcomes shall be in no way hurt by the second death. (Revelation 2:11)

In Revelation 20:14, we are quite unambiguously told that the Lake of Fire is that which constitutes this "second death."

We must give due consideration to the fact Revelation 2:11 is written to the churches and not the world at large. Regardless of what doctrinal positions are held, we are faced with some very pertinent questions. For instance, exactly what kind of relationship does this Lake of Fire have to the white-hot *overcomer*? What relationship does it hold for a *lukewarm believer* or, for that matter, a *cold believer* — which incidentally is a condition our Lord found more desirable? Yet what promise of illumination may it hold for the *unbeliever*, those still blinded by the god of this world? And what incredible relationship will it have with the *adversary* and his *angels* as well as with *death* itself and, conversely, *life*?

Prayerfully, we will explore the answers to these questions either directly or indirectly through inescapable implication. First, I believe it is important to state that I cannot view Revelation 2:11 as merely being a superfluous statement made to the overcomer. Aside from the strong witness I have in the Spirit, the overall structure of God's Word is much more exacting than that! On the surface, the implication of this verse is that in spite of the overcomer's exposure, the fire shall not in any way harm him. For, without actual exposure, the statement "in no way" becomes meaningless! However, in light of the counsel of the totality of God's Word, I believe there is something even deeper to be seen.

On the likeness of the throne *was* a likeness
in appearance like a man on it from above.

And I saw *Him*, like the color of polished bronze,
looking like fire within it all around.
From the appearance of His loins and upward,
and from the appearance of His loins and downward,
I saw *Him* looking like fire; and brightness to it all around.

Ezekiel 1:26–27
Literal Translation

A Flaming Fire

They said to one another, "Was not our heart burning in us as He spoke to us in the highway, and as He opened up to us the Scriptures?" (Luke 24:32; Literal Translation)

I have come to see that the reason the Lake of Fire has no effect upon the overcomer is because these individuals have become *completely one with Holy Fire*. Fire has no discernible effect on fire. One flame simply commingles with the other. The select body of people that are referred to as the overcomers is actually the very same substance that constitutes the body of this lake — just as it is common for us to refer to the greater body of people in the world as "the sea of humanity."

These holy saints have had the purifying effect of the fire worked throughout every aspect of their being. They have entered into the hundredfold realm of the fullness of atonement. "I and the Father" become one in His purpose and also in the exercise of His authority: *sonship* (a relationship not dependent on one's physical gender).

Our mutual exercise of His authority becomes evident when you ponder the real implications of the *union* exposited in John 17, while keeping in mind that "Our God is a consuming fire."

Psalms 104:4 states that "He makes His angels [messengers] spirits, His ministers a *flaming fire*."

And Proverbs 20:27 tells us "The spirit of man is the lamp of Jehovah searching all the inward parts of the heart."

Jesus, being the "true light which, coming into the world, enlightens every man" will perfect a work of enlightenment first in the overcomer. Then by proxy, it will flare up in all those with whom the overcomer comes in contact. Fire spreads! The fullness of the unquenchable Spirit of the Lord given *without measure* illuminates and appropriately deals with every hidden motivation of the heart, whether of sin or of righteousness. Therefore, a single overcoming son of God can be considered a holy flame of living fire.

However, when you take into account all of the overcoming sons together, this will create and constitute a vast all-consuming Lake of Fire.

> His head and His hair were white, like white wool, like snow; and His eyes were like a flame of fire. His feet were like burnished bronze, when it has been made to glow in a furnace, and His voice was like the sound of many waters. (Revelation 1:14-15)

Head and body — this *glorious many-membered Christ* will speak in one unified voice and shall stand as an awesome flaming furnace of righteous judgment.

> Or do you not know that *the saints will judge the world*? If the world is judged by you, are you not competent to constitute the smallest law courts? *Do you not know that we will judge angels*? (1 Corinthians 6:2-3; italics mine)

First Timothy 4:10 clearly defines for us the overcomer's purpose as well as his orientation in the plan of God: "It is for this we labor and strive, because we have fixed our hope on the living God who is the Savior of all men especially of believers."

"Especially of believers?" Not exclusively? All men? What's up with this unwavering hope for *all* through God? So how does He save those who have not come to believe?

> And I saw the dead, the small and the great, standing before God, and books were opened. And another book was opened which is the Book of Life. And the dead were judged out of the things written in the books, according to their works. And the sea gave up the dead in it. And death and hell gave up the dead in them. And they were each judged according to their works. And death and hell were thrown into the Lake of Fire. *This is the second death.* And if anyone was not found having been written in the Book of Life, *he was thrown into the Lake of Fire.*" (Revelation 20:12-15; italics mine)

Because the judgments of man's fleshly natural mind are predominately punitive in nature, they have therefore become the filter through which God's Word has been distorted. By the inherited predisposition of the natural mind, the very word *judgment* has acquired a bad rap. The fact that acquittal is also judgment goes virtually unnoticed. At the core of this bias is the self-serving carnal mind that will always demand his pound of flesh from someone, somewhere, somehow. This is all that the natural mind is capable of understanding. Its brutish logic goes something like:

18

You've hurt me, and now I'm going to make you pay for it! Who cares if there's nothing constructive about it? Somehow my twisted little self just feels better knowing that you've gotten yours!

This, my friends, is exactly the shrunken mentality that organized religion projected (perhaps unwittingly) upon God. However, regardless of how dark a brush others have used to paint our Father, all of God's judgments will forever remain remedial. *They are always corrective and restorative.* All of our Father's destructions must be understood in the overarching context of the fact that He is a *creator*!

> But the vessel that he was making of clay was spoiled in the hand of the potter; so he remade it into another vessel, as it pleased the potter to make. (Jeremiah 18:4)

Praise God that our Father is delightfully consistent in His dealings with humanity! Jesus made it abundantly clear to us that "the word which you hear is not mine, but the Father's who sent me. As I hear, I judge; and my judgment is just because I do not seek my own will but the will of Him who sent me." Forearmed with this understanding, the following scripture reveals not only the abject poverty of our carnal thinking but also the richness of our Father's nobility!

> But I say to you *who hear*: Love your enemies, do good to those who hate you, bless those who curse you, pray for those who mistreat you. Whoever hits you on the cheek, offer him the other also; and whoever takes away your coat, do not withhold your shirt from him either. Give to everyone who asks of you, and whoever takes away what is yours, do not demand it back. Treat others the same way you want them to treat you. *If you love those who love you, what credit is that to you? For even sinners love those who love them. If you do good to those who do good to you, what credit is that to you? For even sinners do the same.* (Luke 6:27-33; italics mine)

> "My thoughts are not your thoughts, nor are your ways my ways," declares the Lord. (Isaiah 55:8)

We are told that "death and hell" (actually death and the grave) and all those who have proven by *the character of their works* to be void of the life of the Lamb are to be cast into the Lake of Fire. But how few understand that here every remaining aspect of their fallen carnal nature will be passionately consumed in God's Holy Fire of living energy. Death and every lifeless work of that realm may enter into the lake, but only the life that has been imparted in the fiery judgments of the Lamb and His overcomers can come out.

> If any man's work is burned up, he will suffer loss; but he himself will be saved, *yet so as through fire*. (1 Corinthians 3:15; italics mine)

Even the angels and their works will be judged in this purifying manner! This fiery process shall continue until every single aspect of death's realm is swallowed up in the all-encompassing, life-giving victory of Christ!

> When all things are subjected to Him, then the Son Himself also will be subjected to the One who subjected all things to Him, so that God may be *all in all*. (1 Corinthians 15:28; italics mine)

Please take note of the fact that this verse does not read *all in some* but all in all. Only when every created thing that has ever been contrary or adversarial to the life of Christ is brought into perfect alignment, thereby becoming an extension of Christ, will the Son then become the perfectly unified expression and extension of the Father. Everything that God has ever created shall ultimately find its rightful place in an ever expanding government of peace. When all things are summed up in Christ (Ephesians 1:10), only then shall God be everything in everyone!

Yet if the Lake of Fire serves the accomplishing of this, it does beg the question, *what aspect of us can die even after we die* (i.e., *second death*)? For the time being, let us remember that I have posed the question, and we shall come back and explore this issue shortly.

We need to realize that in the culture of the first century, when the scroll the Revelation of Jesus Christ was penned by the apostle John, both "fire and brimstone" (fire and sulfur) were commonly known by everyday folk as agents of purification. Therefore, those who were raised in the wisdom of the day would only interpret the archaic idiom "a lake burning with fire and brimstone" as a lake of purification. The Greek language bares this out:

Concordance reference—G4442 fire

pur
Thayer's definition:
   1. fire
   Part of Speech: noun neuter
Pur is the Greek root word from which we get our English word purify.

20

Even in our modern culture, we employ the tool of fire for the very same reason. We use the high heat of an autoclave to purify the instruments used in surgery, thus rendering them free from contagion and safe for use.

Prefiguring the Lake of Fire in type and shadow, it is recorded for us in the book of Numbers that the Hebrew people were instructed to *purify* all of the spoils (treasure) acquired through conquest, *first by fire and then by water*. At this point, it might be very interesting for us to note that the title *overcomer* means "victorious conqueror." I strongly suggest that in God's economy, it is only fitting that these conquerors should make a spoil of every blood-bought soul helplessly harangued and possessed by the vanquished adversary.

Concordance reference—G2303 brimstone

theion
Thayer's definition:
 1. brimstone
 1a. divine incense, because burning brimstone was regarded as
 having power to purify and to ward of disease.
 Part of Speech: noun neuter
Theion is derived from theios, meaning, godlike . . . divinity.

Although it would later prove to be pseudoscience, alchemists would evolve these commonly held ideas of purification. Through a rather immature understanding, they had come to believe that base metals such as tin, copper, and lead could be *purified into gold* through various applications of fire and brimstone.

For those of the Christian community in the first century, our concept of eternal torment as it is preached today would be completely foreign. It is very doubtful they would know of what we were speaking. Most likely, it would elicit the astonished response, "Are you mad?" A little unbiased research into what actually was taught for the first three hundred years of church history would be a real "eye-opener" for many. However, regarding this, I invite you to do your own research for then your findings will have real meaning to you!

It is the glory of God to conceal a matter, but the glory of kings is to search out a matter. (Proverbs 25:2)

Carnal Thinking: Natural or Unnatural?

Were I to say something like "I smell a rat," or "We're on a wild-goose chase," to those who have grown up in American culture, they would readily understand my meaning. Although, to a foreigner, these same idioms are totally baffling. Anyone who has grown up isolated from our culture has a total loss for understanding this type of speech. The reason for this is that they have no choice other than to take the words literally. Rather than fostering the intended communication within the minds of these listeners, my words are far more likely to prompt them to begin sniffing at the air with disdain, or wishing that they had put on their running shoes. They would simply have no frame of reference for the subtle pictures that are being painted beyond the words.

Our modern Western culture is isolated from the pen of the apostle John by 1,900 years and by language barriers and foreign cultural idioms. Not to mention the fact that the book, known by the truncated title of Revelation, declares itself right from the gate (Revelation 1:1) to be a book that was communicated through *signs* and/or *symbols*. Truly, apart from the mind of Christ, we have no frame of reference to understand the beautiful word pictures that have been painted for us.

> Blessed [*happy*, G3107] is he who reads and blessed [*happy*, G3107] are those who listen to the words of this prophecy and lay to heart what is written in it; for the time for its fulfillment is now close at hand. (Revelation 1:3)

If the glorious Revelation of Jesus Christ (salvation) fosters fear, apprehension, or dread, it is only because the carnal mind, being devoid of understanding, is engaged in projecting fearful images upon the screen of the mind. Convincing imagery, for which the mind has no reference point, must therefore be interpreted literally. But then, the carnal mind can only walk by its physical sight, so all of this is quite natural and to be expected.

I am fully persuaded that the reason the book of Revelation is presented in such beautifully cryptic code is the very same reason that Jesus spoke in parables. That is specifically so it could not be accurately understood by what is called the natural mind! But as I know how such a statement is an affront to the natural ego-driven mind, please "do have a go of it" yourself.

> And He was saying, "He who has ears to hear, let him hear." As soon as He was alone, His followers, along with the twelve, began asking Him about the parables. And He was saying to them, "To you has been given the mystery of the Kingdom of God, but those who are outside get everything in parables so that *while seeing, they may see and not perceive; and while hearing, they may hear and not understand, otherwise they might return and be forgiven*." And He said to them, "*Do you not understand this parable*? How will you understand all the parables?" (Mark 4:9-13; italics mine)

Incredible, is it not? "Otherwise they might return and be forgiven." I'd be willing to bet that you thought that was the whole idea! Yet this is the very same reason that we are told in the book of beginnings:

> Then the Lord God said, "Behold, the man has become like one of Us, knowing good and evil; and now, he might stretch out his hand, and take also from the tree of life, and eat, and live forever." (Genesis 3:22)
>
> So He drove the man out; and at the east of the garden of Eden He stationed the cherubim and the flaming sword which turned every direction to guard the way to the tree of life. (Genesis 3:24)

We really need to establish at the very core of our understanding the fact that *there is no salvation for the fleshly natural mind, will, and emotions*. There wasn't any in the garden, there isn't now, nor will there ever be! In order to partake of the Tree of Life, we must submit our fleshly mind to this flaming sword. Only those who have been willing to lose their head for Christ's sake will ever experience the mind of Christ!

It is the destiny of the carnal mind to be utterly consumed by fire. This will either be affected voluntarily in this life, or it shall be imposed by an immersion in the Lake of Fire! In regard to this *baptism*, the titles *believer*, *unbeliever*, or *overcomer* are absolutely meaningless—all shall be *salted with fire*! However, honor, privilege, and station shall be determined by how and under what circumstance this is accomplished! When we were told, "flesh and blood shall not inherit the Kingdom of God," it was not talking about the skin we are in, so much as the state of mind we are temporarily in!

> Blessed and holy is the one who has a part in *the first resurrection; over these the second death has no power*, but they will be priests of God and of Christ and will reign with Him for a thousand years. (Revelation 20:6; italics mine)

Remember that those who have the honor to take part in the first resurrection do so only because they have attained unto a *prize*. This inestimable blessing is not the automatic result of having received the "free gift" of atonement. It is because beyond accepting the Father's loving provision, they counted the cost according to Luke 14:25-35 and joyfully reordered all of the priorities of their lives. Through this action, they became willing to pay the price.

If I am not coming across in this as Dr. Feel-Good, it really cannot be helped; we have been misled by comfortable religious fables and lied to long enough! It is necessary that the veil over our mind created by the precepts of men be torn asunder! Father's Spirit assures us that in the end we will be eternally grateful for the boldness of the truth that sets us free! For only in Truth shall we be free indeed!

> Whoever then annuls one of the least of these commandments, and teaches others to do the same, shall be called least in the kingdom of heaven; but whoever keeps and teaches them, he shall be called great in the kingdom of heaven. (Matthew 5:19)

There are certain foundational precepts of which we may be fully assured. The natural, although highly religious, mind will never possess an ear that is attuned to hearing God's Spirit. Nor will the natural mind ever possess a consciousness that can dynamically see into the depth of our Father's love. Yet perhaps most crucial for us is the fact that it is not possible for this mind to speak of the things of God without entering into gross error. Incidentally, the popular idea that a *lukewarm believer* is someone who has become ambivalent about the things of God is patently false! These believers have a tremendous zeal for God, but it is not according to a true relational knowledge. Their puffed-up religious carnality believes itself the possessor of a rich understanding, and with a close relationship, but all that they think they possess shall in the end prove to be illusion!

> Because you say, "I am rich, and have become wealthy, and have need of nothing," and you do not know that you are wretched and miserable and poor and blind and naked. (Revelation 3:17)

Seven times in the opening chapters of the Revelation of Jesus Christ we read, "He who has an ear, let him hear what the Spirit says to the churches." The profound implication of this is that within the "called" there are *many* who have not developed ears that can actually hear. The *few* that are "chosen" are they who have developed what our Lord has called a hearing ear, which is only proven in their continual response to the Spirit's direction.

Please examine what I now say very carefully. Only those who have been *willing* to lose their head (own intellect, will, and personal feelings) for Christ's sake will experience the mind of Christ! Furthermore, it is only because *new spiritual faculties* are imparted through this experience that any are able to hear and receive vital direction for their lives.

Through the impartation of these new abilities, these individuals go on to overcome *all* influence of the world what remains of their fleshly mind and the devil. They are enabled to walk above that realm even while yet being in it. Continually hearing their Master's voice, they follow the Lamb wherever He goes. Of these overcomers, Isaiah also prophesied,

> Behold, a king will reign righteously and princes will rule justly. Each will be like a refuge from the wind and a shelter from the storm, like streams of water in a dry country, like the shade of a huge rock in a parched land. *Then* the eyes of those who see will not be blinded, and the ears of those who hear will listen. The mind of the hasty will discern the truth, and the tongue of the stammers will hasten to speak clearly. *No longer will the fool be called noble, or the rogue be spoken of as generous, for a fool speaks nonsense, and his heart inclines toward wickedness: To practice ungodliness and to speak error against the Lord, to keep the hungry person unsatisfied and to withhold drink from the thirsty.* (Isaiah 32:1-6; italics mine)

Jesus tried His best to point out the inherent weakness of man's untrustworthy mind when He said,

> A blind man cannot guide a blind man, can he?
> Will they not both fall into a pit? (Luke 6:39)

The fleshly natural mind of man is not only blind; it is altogether blind to its own blindness! Thus, ignorance squared is responsible for the great many distortions that have found their way into the pit that is commonly called organized religion. Moreover, the mountain of confusion that blind guides have created in our culture has been compounded even further by well-documented biased translation of the scriptures.

> How can you say, "We are wise, and the law of the *Lord* is with us"? But *behold, the lying pen of the scribes has made it into a lie.* "The wise men are put to shame, they are dismayed and caught; behold, they have rejected the word of the *Lord*, and what kind of wisdom do they have?" (Jeremiah 8:8-9; italics mine)

The history of Bible translation is replete with examples of people playing fast and loose with the meaning of words and imposing the bias of an agenda that comes way short of the glory of God!

Now, does this mean that we can't trust God's Word? No, it does not mean that at all! Clearly, it does mean we should not trust man's word! We have a profound responsibility not to *blindly* accept man's word for God's Word where it has forced its way on to the printed page! To throw the baby out with the dirty bathwater is the lazy cop-out reaction of the fleshly mind!

This literary chicanery does hold profound implications for us, in that some of the things we may have signed off on are suspect! If this is ever pointed out, we have all along had the standing orders to "prove all things." Only the manipulation of a carnal religious order would ever encourage us to accept doctrine without questioning its validity. Truly, I tell you, have no faith in anything that cannot stand up to scrutiny!

I pray along with our brother Paul that "the eyes of your heart would be enlightened so that you might truly know what is the hope of His

26

calling," and in addition, that you would come to realize that any call on your life was never personal! Our call has always been on behalf of a suffering mankind.

The *wisdom of God* shall only be found through a willingness to keep our own understanding upon the altar, there to be continually tried and validated in the light of God's full counsel.

Jesus established the necessity for humility in this matter when He said,

> If you were blind, you would have no sin; but since *you say*, "We see," your sin remains. (John 9:41)

Whenever a man, while being honestly
mistaken, hears the truth, either
that man ceases to be mistaken or
henceforth is no longer honest!

(Authorship unknown)

God's Fire: Creative Purpose or Pointless Terror?

To this very day, a falsehood known as *eternal damnation* has been associated with these particular verses about the Lake of Fire. But these spurious ideas wouldn't find their way into Christianity until around two hundred years after the apostle penned the Revelation of Jesus Christ.

In 312 CE, Emperor Constantine would march his pagan legions under the sign of the cross and would *Christianize* them en masse. In 313 CE, Christianity (which up to that time had been an outlawed religion) became officially sanctioned by the state. This seemingly generous action would stimulate a great influx of people into the ranks of the church, but it is this tide of people that would bring their pagan concepts of the underworld into Christianity (a subterranean world ruled by the gods Orcus, Erebus, Tartarus, and Infernus or Inferna whence comes our expression "infernal regions"). This blurring of lines of demarcation between pagan and Christian would continue under an atmosphere of tolerance for ideas in a bid to unify a fragmenting Roman Empire.

Lo and behold, Constantine's ecumenical ploy worked. The Holy Roman Empire was born out of this unholy marriage of the Kingdom of God with the worldly kingdom of men. This horrendous union would soon prove a recipe for great abuse!

By retaining an appearance of godliness, yet denying the saving power, the light was obscured. The sad result was an inexorable slide into a period of intense wickedness that would come to be called the Dark Ages.

These historical subjects are truly fascinating and are altogether worthy of personal study. Therefore, I pray this appetizer would only stir your *pure mind's* hunger.

For now, our mutual purpose is to explore His fiery presence in our present "age of grace." We need to come to understand how God is actively working to consume all that would offend in the soulish realm of our makeup.

Know this: The *soul* of man *is* an extremely precious commodity in the sight of God. Our Father paid an awesome price for the full redemption of every man's spirit, soul, and body. He personally has a vested interest in every person!

Second Corinthians 5:19 says, "God was in Christ reconciling the world to Himself, not counting their trespasses against them, and He has committed to us the word of reconciliation."

Good News

The good news we have been *commissioned to proclaim* is that no man, from Adam until the close of time, will ever have to pay a debt that has already been paid on his behalf!

My brethren, this is some real foot-stomping, hallelujah-singing, God-praising

good news!

 Yet a dysfunctional wonder known as organized religion has by and large sold to the masses *a god that somehow has changed his mind*. Because to hear them tell it, *God is counting the world's trespasses against them*, willing to send them to some fabled hellhole. They have completely forgotten that long ago, their own darkened minds concocted this ghoulish fiction.

These are the scheming wordsmiths that we trusted to translate the Greek into Latin and the Latin into the King's English.

You might ask, why would God allow this to happen?

Because they did not receive the love of the truth so as to be saved. For this reason God will send upon them a deluding influence so that they will believe what is false, in order that they all may be judged who did not believe the truth, but took pleasure in wickedness. (2 Thessalonians 2:10-12)

The apostle Paul speaking prophetically:

I know that after my departure, savage wolves will come in among you, *not sparing the flock*; and from *among your own selves men will arise, speaking perverse things*, to draw away the disciples after them. (Acts 20:29-30; italics mine)

How easily people turn a blind eye to the fact that the conscious manipulation of people and circumstances is the definition of witchcraft. Unscrupulous, power-hungry church leaders, capitalizing on latent seeds of pagan thought, have used tactics such as the doctrine of hell to frighten spiritually immature children into obedience. This doctrine was engineered by carnal minds for the sole purpose of controlling the masses through terror!

However, these manipulative tactics of terror will never hold a candle to the internal motivation of love. For it is love alone that creates a genuine and overwhelming desire to do our Father's will. It is solely the goodness of God that leads anyone to true and lasting repentance.

No!

A lie can never become truth, even were it to enjoy universal acceptance!

It seems that the Spirit would have me beat this drum loudly because this truly is a travesty of monumental proportions! The doctrine of hell has maligned the nature of God and the purpose of His Holy Fire long enough!

For approximately one thousand years, the truth concerning salvation by faith in Christ's redemptive work was withheld from the understanding of the masses. For more than a millennium, Christianity would labor under a falsehood that a person's own merits or that the indulgences sold by the church would earn them an entrance into the heavenly realm. Upon receipt of monetary payment, the church would extend merit to the sinner by tapping into the "church's treasure house of merit" stored up from the good deeds of the saints. It was a perfect system of servitude to corruption.

On October 31, 1517, the hour came to begin to illumine the darkened consciousness of the church; and Martin Luther nailed his Ninety-five Theses to the door of Castle Church in Wittenberg, Germany. This bold action would come to inaugurate a new era, but it would not completely eradicate the darkness in which the church had shrouded herself.

However, from that time forward all up through to our present day, our Father has sent wave after wave of refreshing life, light, and love. God's Holy Spirit would pour out revival after revival, and each one would bring a fresh and progressive revelation of truth, power, and grace. Yet for all this illumination, the church has continued to labor under the falsehood of the doctrine of hell for another five hundred years. To this very day, Christianity continues to offer an imagined salvation from this fictional place of torment rather than from the curses that were placed upon man's alienated consciousness in Eden.

I believe that an hour has once again come to illumine the awareness of the church, and I am seeing many signs of this happening throughout the world. Correcting the sacrosanct lie known as the doctrine of hell is crucial to the spiritual and physical well-being of not only the church but also of every person on this planet!

Spend a moment if you will, imagine the multibillions of people on this planet, each one of them is pointing an accusing finger at every other person including himself and God. It is none other than the prince accuser himself who rules this dark psychic atmosphere of blame and condemnation. The sorry fruit of the fictitious doctrine of hell is nothing less than a great magnification of the destructive force of his debilitating kingdom of shame. Truly, after six thousand years of dining on our dusty consciousness, the little serpent has grown to be a great dragon! And he deceives the whole world!

> Then I heard a loud voice in heaven, saying, "Now the salvation, and the power, and the kingdom of our God and the authority of His Christ have come, for the accuser of our brethren has been thrown down, he who accuses them before our God day and night." (Revelation 12:10)

The true meaning of the word *forgive* is the giving of a covering charity *before* there is a need. For-giving is why we were told that the Lamb was slain from before the foundation of the world! It is to say, "Lift up your countenance, my friend, you are completely covered by my love! Your faltering steps do not alter the life, light, and love that I hold for you. Now go in peace to realize that you are free!"

> Love is patient, love is kind and is not jealous; love does not brag and is not arrogant, does not act unbecomingly; it does not seek its own, is not provoked, does not take into account a wrong suffered, does not rejoice in unrighteousness, but rejoices with the truth; bears all things, believes all things, hopes all things, endures all things. Love never fails. (1 Corinthians 13:4-8)

God never fails, for *God is love*!

Unconditional love (agape) must have unlovely conditions in order to find any true expression. Indeed, unconditional love cannot be seen for what it is, except against a backdrop of unlovely conditions! God can only display His primal attribute in His response to rebellion!

> For *God has* shut up all in disobedience *so that He may show mercy to all.* Oh, the depth of the riches both of the wisdom and knowledge of God! How unsearchable are His judgments and unfathomable His ways! (Romans 11:32-33; italics mine)

Jesus taught His followers that if you were not willing to forgive men their transgressions, and in truth from your heart, neither could you ever experience the true depth of our Father's forgiveness. You see, by any accounting of debt, we can never come to know the depth of our Father's heart. Yet contained in this "hellish" doctrine of demons is the demand that every last farthing be paid by the people of this world — nothing is forgiven, nothing is covered, the world is held fully accountable.

This damnable doctrine is literally holding the world hostage to fear and degradation! All the while, good people who are called by God's name are totally asleep to their privilege, right, and responsibility to loose these captives by canceling the consciousness of their debt!

> If you remit the sins of any persons, they remain remitted to them. If you bind fast the sins of any, *they* remain bound. (John 20:23; italics mine)

Quite accurately did Mahatma Gandhi observe, "An eye for an eye makes the whole world blind."

It is in this very way that the world is bound over in ignorance, and so it continues on its downward spiral of increasing guilt and shame! Why is it not obvious that hatred, greed, fear, and wars are not born from out of an atmosphere of love and light? Tragically, those who've actually been given the power to affect change do little or nothing in the painful blindness of their religious carnality!

Speaking to the dogmatic carnal mind of the religious, Jesus very pointedly said, "You are experts at setting aside the commandment of God in order to keep your tradition." Today we tend to think of ourselves as being much more sophisticated than that, except that is precisely the problem! Do you seriously think that the blind nature of religious carnality has changed the slightest bit in two thousand years?

Through the unconscionable doctrine of eternal torment, the beauty of the all-encompassing love of God is reduced to little more than a ring of gold in a swine's snout! In a universe of perverse ideas, none exceeds the idea that an Omnipotent Creator called love would consign even one of His children to be eternally tortured! The error in any child may openly be condemned, for this is a manifestation of love! However, no earthly parent not totally deranged and void of natural affection would ever abandon love for his child no matter how egregious the error. Even when parents are estranged from their children, they do still hold a place of love for them. Our collective understanding of God's justice has been twisted in the extreme by partaking of the knowledge of good and evil. Truly, I tell you, those who tenaciously cling to the doctrine of "eternal torment" know not what spirit they are of! Religion not grounded in Truth is such an absolute sham!

The apostle Paul made a very revealing statement when he said in 2 Corinthians 5:16, "From now on, we recognize no one according to the flesh."

The ability to see beyond the world's sinful flesh to the finished work of Christ is an absolute impossibility for those who peddle the doctrine of hell. Thus, they recognize the entire world according to the flesh! By doing so, they are unwittingly bearing false witness against their neighbor! They magnify the mote in their brother's eye all the while they are oblivious to the beam in their own!

Alas, there is a remnant, some of which currently walk the earth. Yet many have passed over into the cloud of witnesses. These have not bowed the knee to the Baal of false religious dogma. Internally they have overcome all need to exact payment for the pain in the world. Joyfully these have come into unity with the forgiving heart of God. They are one in purpose, love, authority, and forgiveness.

Never doubt that a small group of committed people can change the world; indeed, it is the only thing that ever has. (Margaret Meade, world-renown anthropologist)

However, the most credible definition of a biblical remnant that I have ever heard is "a person or persons who fulfill God's purpose on behalf of the whole when the whole either cannot or will not fulfill it."

This definition would make our Lord the ultimate remnant who, being in agony, beheld in a moment of time all of history's slaves to sin and agreed from the cross, "Father, forgive them, for they do not know what they are doing." (Father, I also release them, for all humanity is acting in blind unconsciousness.)

For it is God the Father who so loved in forgiveness that He freely gave us the provision of His only begotten Son!

36

The Hour of Jubilee Approaches!

In this hour, our Lord has a body of people that have grown up, and they continue to grow up into conscious agreement with their Head. Across the pages of time, this body of overcomers has been called out of man's religious systems. These represent an *ekklesia* of sons.

These "sons of God" share in a single consciousness and, when moved at the behest of the Lord, shall fulfill their Father's purpose on behalf of the *whole world*! This glorious manifestation of our Father's love is destined to set *all* of creation free!

> For the anxious longing of the creation waits eagerly for *the revealing of the sons of God*. For the creation was subjected to futility, not willingly, but because of Him who subjected it, in hope that the creation itself also will be set free from its slavery to corruption into the freedom of the glory of the children of God. (Romans 8:19-21; italics mine)

There is a wonderfully illustrative story that goes something like this:

> "Tell me the weight of a snowflake," a hawk implored of a wild dove. "Nothing more than nothing," was the answer. "In that case I must tell you a marvelous story," said the hawk. "I sat on the branch of a fir, close to its trunk. It began to snow, not heavily, not a raging blizzard, no, just like in a dream, without any violence. Since I had nothing better to do, I counted the snowflakes settling on the twigs and needles of my branch. Their number was exactly 3,741,952 when the next snowflake dropped onto the branch—'nothing more than nothing' as you say—and the branch broke off." Having said that, the hawk flew away.
>
> The dove, since Noah's time being an authority on peace, thought about the story for a while and finally said with resolve, "Perhaps only one person's voice is lacking for peace to come about in the world." (Authorship unknown)

While you are marveling over the irony of the hawk instructing the dove, consider for a moment, are you a peacemaker?

Really? Would you be willing to pay back what someone else stole?

Yes, it's designed to be a difficult question. It takes us out of the dreamy realm of idealism we so easily spin about ourselves. The idea of tangibly laying down our life and covering someone else in the cause of peace serves to bring to us some honest perspective.

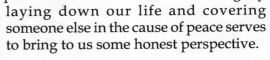

Blessed are the peacemakers, for it is they who will be recognized as sons of God. (Matthew 5:9)

The book of Revelation describes the organized systems of man as being the *highly seductive and beautifully arrayed* "Babylon the Great" (Revelation 17:3-5). This is a carnal dominion or hegemony, threefold in nature, encompassing all of man's *financial, political,* and *religious* systems. These transnational systems are arrayed in an outward appearance that looks good and honorable. Yet their true nature is all manner of abomination: lies, manipulation, greed, and confusion. Man's well-respected systems supply grand utopian promises; yet the carnal mind's finest work will never deliver any financial, political, or religious peace! History testifies to this fact; still it is rare that an individual takes notice. The world's "wool" has so effectively been pulled over their sleepy eyes.

> I heard another voice from heaven, saying, "Come out of her, my people, so that you will not participate in her sins and *receive of her plagues*." (Revelation 18:4; italics mine)

Truth is "the earth is the Lord's and everything in it," and stamped upon every bit of it is "not guilty" — account paid in full! The only question is, what draconian measures will it take for our Father to break the hypnotic trance of carnality and *shake* this world fully *awake* to the *truth* of it?

The freely given gift of every man's redemption is already a fully accomplished (finished) fact! It was accomplished at Calvary two thousand years ago. The entire Adamic race died on the cross in Jesus as the last Adam gave up his spirit. A new will and testament was written in His precious blood! This testament guarantees our life and peace for it takes precedence over our old inheritance of death and decay! Every single person shall have the veracity of this ransom testified to in their appointed time (1 Timothy 2:6).

Unfortunately, for the time being, it appears that some of the heirs of this new will and testament are incommunicado with the executor of the estate. But even this sorry state of affairs can never disqualify any for the benefit of the gift.

> For the gifts and the calling of God are irrevocable. (Romans 11:29)

However, I am sure we agree that no one may enjoy any benefit until actually receiving the "free gift" of His work.

It is according to God's purpose that in our present "graceful age," a few souls are *gently being enlightened* into a saving faith in Christ. We find this stated in the following scripture:

> *In the exercise of His will* He brought us forth by the word of truth, so that we would be a kind of first fruits among His creatures. (James 1:18; italics mine)

The term *first fruits* portends the full harvest in the age to come! However, the balance of humanity will not be gently awakened. This harvest of souls will suddenly have their darkened understanding destroyed in the undimmed glory of His redemptive work!

Consider the all-encompassing scope of Christ's work, in that He

> went and made proclamation to the spirits now in prison, who once were disobedient, when the patience of God kept waiting in the days of Noah, during the construction of the ark, in which a few, that is eight persons, were brought safely through the water. (1 Peter 3:19-20)

> For the gospel has for this purpose been preached even to those who are dead, that though they are judged in the flesh as men, they may live in the spirit according to the will of God. (1 Peter 4:6)

The inconvenient truth of these verses clearly flies in the face of the extrabiblical nonsense that salvation is only available in this earthly realm. According to this, Jesus has even proclaimed liberty, by virtue of His atonement, to those spirits whose souls were so helplessly wicked that our Father saw fit that it was best to start anew! Jesus has led captive the entire host of captives in every realm! Preach the everlasting gospel!

> And I saw another angel flying in midheaven, having *an eternal gospel* to preach to those who live on the earth, and to every nation and tribe and tongue and people. (Revelation 14:6; italics mine)

Jesus said that only *the attributing of the work of the Holy Spirit to the adversary* (blasphemy) would not be forgiven in the age to come. Everything else would be completely covered at that time by what was about to take place at Calvary! This is why He is called the Savior of all men, but especially of those who believe.

> Therefore I say to you, any sin and blasphemy shall be forgiven people, but blasphemy against the Spirit shall not be forgiven. Whoever speaks a word against the Son of Man, it shall be forgiven him; but whoever speaks against the Holy Spirit, it shall not be forgiven him, either in this age [law] or in the age to come [grace]. (Matthew 12:31-32)

40

Because of the tremendous amount of fear and misunderstanding surrounding these verses, I am compelled to address this. *Our Father is not now, nor will He ever hold anything against you or anyone else for that matter!* This so-called SIN is totally self-inflicted nonsense.

If I may illustrate what I mean: in order for any person to speak a word against God's Holy Spirit, one must first of necessity have misidentified our "helper" as being our enemy (adversary) (Matthew 12:24). *By doing this, we have cut off our own conscious awareness* from the only provision of love, forgiveness, and guidance that exists in the universe. Now, being estranged from the only flow of life that exists, do you really think that any such person would be up to the task of successfully navigating this mortal realm (*realm of death*)? It could be that some people have convinced themselves they will be the first to accomplish it on the strength of their own religious prowess. Maybe they have actually come to think of their own thoughts as being the Holy Spirit. Whatever the case, Jesus addressed this condition when He said, "If the light that is in you is darkness, how great is that darkness?" This topsy-turvy situation can only find its corrective judgment in the age-lasting Lake of Fire where that *which maketh a lie* will no longer have any choice but to die out unto life eternal (i.e., second death).

> For as in Adam *all* die, *so also* in Christ *all* will be made alive. (1 Corinthians 15:22; italics mine)

There is an awesome truth expressed in this verse, and it is presented to us as a mathematical equation. The phrase *so also* is the equivalent of a verbal equal (=) sign.

For as in Adam *100 percent die, so also in Christ 100 percent* shall be made alive.

> But each in his own order: Christ the first fruits, after that those who are Christ's at His coming, then comes the end, when He hands over the kingdom to the God and Father, when He has abolished all rule and all authority and power. (1 Corinthians 15:23-24)

Each in his own order was typified in Israel's harvest feasts:

1. *Christ the first fruits*	Passover	Barley Harvest
2. *Those who are Christ's at His coming*	Pentecost	Wheat Harvest
3. *Then comes the end* (last order)	Tabernacles	Wine and Oil Harvest

41

Then I looked, and a white cloud appeared, and sitting on the cloud was some One resembling the Son of Man, having a wreath of gold upon His head and in His hand a sharp sickle. (Revelation 14:14)

The right to consciously walk in the awesome blessing of our inheritance was not even acquired by us until that precious moment when we first perceived and accepted what had already been done. When we saw the magnitude of the love that had finished on our behalf, what we could never do for ourselves, our soul spontaneously responded and confessed that Jesus Christ is Lord. One day, every knee is destined to see these wondrous truths and spontaneously bow in adoration. Revelation 5:13 gloriously proclaims the adoration of all.

And every created thing which is in heaven and on the earth and under the earth and on the sea, and all things in them, I heard saying, "To Him who sits on the throne, and to the Lamb, be blessing and honor and glory and dominion forever and ever." (Revelation 5:13)

In our personal moment of confession, *our spirit*, realizing its inheritance, was "born from above."

But the Jerusalem above is free; she is our mother. (Galatians 4:26)

In joy, we were brought forth from an incorruptible realm of perfection. This experience is uniquely precious to each of us when the living flame of God's Spirit brought life to our temple, the chains of our darkness being consumed in the fire of His love.

Yet our gloriously illuminated spirit continues as seated (established) in a heavenly realm. This is a timeless realm of authority and truth, not a geographical place. For Jesus, seated in our spirit, is Lord of lords, the rightful governor of *His habitation — we are bought with a price, and we are not our own!*

When the victorious Savior of the World stepped forth from an impotent tomb, He did so, holding the title deed for the earth of our body, the heavens of our soul, and the life of our spirit.

Our Savior is altogether worthy to loose the seals of this deed, which had previously been given over to adversity!

> And He is an atoning sacrifice for our sins, and not for ours only, but also for the sins of the whole world. (1 John 2:2)

Jesus said in Mark 8:34-37,

> Whoever desires to come after Me, let him deny himself and take his cross, and let him follow Me. For *whoever desires to save his life, he shall lose it.* But whoever shall lose his life for My sake and the gospel; *that one shall save it.* For what shall it profit a man if he gain the whole world, yet forfeit his soul? Or what shall a man give as an exchange for his soul? (Italics mine)

Herein lies the answer to what aspect of us can *die* even *after we die.* Incidentally, this also is why the overcomer shall be in no way hurt by the second death. He simply has nothing more to lose . . . every *sacrifice* shall be salted with salt (preserved).

> And do not fear those who kill the body, but cannot kill the soul; but rather fear him who is able to destroy both soul and body in Gehenna. (Matthew 10:28)

The word that has been translated (abstracted) as hell in most English translations of this verse is the Hebrew proper noun "Gehenna." Gehenna is an actual place in ancient Israel. Gehenna is the valley in the Old Testament called ga ben Hinnom or the valley of the son of Hinnom. Gehenna was a place where the environment received a cleansing, where worthless rubbish was burned up. It was *Jerusalem's city dump*!

Considering the awesome price our Father was willing to pay for our redemption, what could Jesus have possibly been saying in Matthew 10:28?

To gain a clear perspective here, we need to realize that at no time did Jesus ever say this to the multitudes; instead, this was only spoken privately *to His disciples.*

Primarily, Jesus was addressing man's out-of-balance fear of man. Men have the tendency to give more respect to man whom they can see than to God whom they cannot see. Jesus is reminding them that the body, being a temporary arrangement, like the grass of the field is here today and tomorrow is burned in the oven. So don't be overly concerned with what man can physically do to you. In this, we do not see any big news flash that our bodies are destroyed. But what exactly is it about our soul that our Father could consider to be so worthless that He would be willing to accelerate its destruction in fire, as this reference, to Gehenna would indicate?

A Rags-to-Riches Story

Only a *transformed soul* has the right to the Tree of Life!

> Blessed are those who wash their robes, so that they may have the right to the Tree of Life, and may enter by the gates into the city. (Revelation 22:14)

The washing of one's robe, the renewing of one's mind, or the putting off the old man and putting on the new all refer in figurative language and are symbolic of the *conversion* or *transformation* of the soul.

> That in reference to your former manner of life, you lay aside the old self, which is being corrupted in accordance with the lusts of deceit, and that you be renewed in the spirit of your mind, and put on the new self, which in the likeness of God has been created in righteousness and holiness of the truth. (Ephesians 4:22-24)

This putting on of the new self is the meaning that is behind the phrase "work out your salvation." The *salvation* of the dimension of man referred to as his "soul" is a process of renewal, and it is only worked out over the course of a believer's life.

> Obtaining as the outcome of your faith the salvation of your souls. (1 Peter 1:9)

I feel it is important to stress that we are not working *for* our *salvation*!

> For it is by grace that you have been saved through faith; and that not of yourselves. It is God's gift, and is not on the ground of merit so that it may be impossible for any one to boast. (Ephesians 2:8-9)

But this *gift* pertains to the *spirit* beings that we are! In contradistinction to this, the salvation of man's *soul* (mind, will, and emotion) is only procured as the outcome of a successful walk in faith. This portion of God's redemptive program is not by any means a gift; it is a race against time for the prize of our own transformed souls!

> You were running well; who hindered you from obeying the truth? (Galatians 5:7)

In this, we come face-to-face with a problem because people have misidentified their mind as the being that they are. Most have actually come to believe that they are their thoughts. This, however, is only a fictional identity. It is known as the ego, and it is the creation of the carnal mind. It is a selfhood that is totally illegitimate. In other words, it is a walking-talking lie that has been fathered by the "father of lies."

It was the egocentric identity in the Pharisees that Jesus was addressing when He told them that they were of their father, the devil. Another strong example of this would be Jesus' response to Peter when He equated man's self-centered agenda with Satan.

> But turning around and seeing His disciples, He rebuked Peter and said, "Get behind Me, Satan; for you are not setting your mind on God's interests, but man's." (Mark 8:33)

Jesus emphatically told us that if we desired to be His disciple, we must deny the validity of this imaginary selfhood that truly has no right to exist.

Once again, we are a spirit being. Our spirit has been enrobed in our soul, exactly as our body would wear a suit of clothes. The spirit wears the dimension of the soul just as the soul wears the dimension of the body. The profound biblical implications of this will become increasingly evident as we proceed.

Now, brethren, let us put on the new man!

For in an untransformed condition, the finest possessions of our Soul are as soiled rags, compared to the Spotless Bride in Light JESUS pines for.

Romans 12:2 instructs us to

> not follow the customs of the present age, but *be transformed by the entire renewal of your minds*, so that you may learn by experience what God's

will is — that will which is good and beautiful and perfect. (Weymouth New Testament; italics mine)

The beautiful sentiment in this verse is full of promise. Although, I think we all agree, it is a bit easier to read this scripture than to live it out. Why do you suppose this might be?

For one thing, I believe *we are clueless* when it comes to understanding the extent to which we have been conditioned by and unconsciously conformed to the "customs of the present age." We are largely unaware of what constitutes the customs that are so damaging to our awareness of God's presence. Neither do I believe we comprehend the mechanics of how we became so susceptible to worldly influence, nor what we may currently be doing to perpetuate these conditions. So in a word, we're clueless!

The remainder of this small book is dedicated to addressing these issues in a way that prayerfully will help to facilitate our individual process of transformation. At the very least, it may help many to gain a fuller understanding about ourselves in this *dynamic living relationship with our Father*.

Transformation: A Fiery Process

The conversion of the soul is a fiery process that takes place over time as the consciousness or the awareness of the mind of Christ is formed in us. However, this awareness can only be formed in those who are willing to lose their own egocentric life.

> My children, with whom I am again in labor until Christ is formed in you. (Galatians 4:19)

Although there may be times that this process will seem less than joyful, there will be other times when we will find a great deal of satisfaction in consciously cooperating with the mind of His Spirit. Whether the road we walk is smooth or rough, the captain of our salvation is having His way with us, for He is "the author and the finisher of our faith." I should also add that the road is only as rough as we have unwittingly decided to make it. "It is hard to kick against the goads." For although it is true that one of the ways a person can learn to make good decisions is by sometimes making a whole series of bad ones, this perhaps is not the preferable path to take. However, this is a well-worn path that we all seem to walk to one degree or another.

The real power of transformation is in learning to be led exclusively by His Spirit while *rejecting* the capriciousness of *our own personal* (including religious) *opinions, attitudes, ideas, and beliefs.* Admittedly, learning to question the validity of our thoughts and feelings is something that does not come easy for us. Casting down these cherished imaginings from the heavens of our mind feels like we are dying. Indeed, it is true we are dying. In humility, we are losing our life for His sake.

At one time, we freely walked according to the course of this world's ordered arrangement. Now this has changed because the former order of *body-soul-spirit* has become *spirit-soul-body.*

Formerly, our soul could happily follow the sensual dictates of the body. Our spirit, being dead in trespasses and sins, could have no say in the matter; for the dead are nonresponsive. Now, however, we find the soul in a crisis, for in our regenerated spirit dwells His living and active Spirit of holiness. Because of the fact that he that is joined to the Lord is one Spirit, we shall find it convicting our personal little world of both sin and of righteousness! I, burning in the midst of you, am mighty! *Hallelujah!* Thank you, Lord!

48

It is essential that we acknowledge that *he* is Lord of all! Or else be honest enough to realize that we are not honoring Him as Lord and repent! If we have truly made Him the Lord of our life, we gave up all right to self-determination! Behold, the "bondslave of the Lord!" Surprisingly, His lordship extends into areas that we may have never considered.

We must realize that He is Lord over every aspect of our life, even over those areas where we are tempted to make our own determination about how far we may have fallen short. We are learning in this that we do not even have the right to point a condemning finger at ourselves, let alone anyone else! One instant, He will use us as a vessel of honor. In the next, to our great vexation, we will discover ourselves being used as a vessel of dishonor. Humiliating? Maybe. Humbling? Absolutely! Get over it!

This is happening for our ultimate edification. It is part of the shaping and molding process as the Master Potter spins us around in various circumstances for His own purposes. Through it all, He is clearly exposing us to our facades. I ask you, how well did Peter know himself when he told the Lord, "I will never deny you"? This same type of fiery purging onto humility is being accomplished in all the brethren as He works all things after the counsel of His own will.

Trust Him! Learn of Him! Be transformed in the fire!

Then Shadrach, Meshach, and Abed-nego came forth of the midst of the fire.

Union: The Two Shall Be One

If you have ever found yourself wondering what our Father is up to through all of these intense dealings, I would tell you that He is still on plan A.

> And God said, "Let Us make man in Our image, according to Our likeness." (Genesis 1:26)

First Corinthians 6:17 tells us that "he that is joined to the Lord is one Spirit!" Now, I know that this is a mind-numbing thought, but there is no point at which we can make a division between our spirit and His Spirit. His Spirit has actually been infused into our spirit. He has filled us with Himself.

> But the King will answer them, "In solemn truth I tell you that in so far as you rendered such services to one of the humblest of these my brethren, you rendered them to myself." (Matthew 25:40; Weymouth New Testament)

Therefore, *irrespective of our physical gender,* our spirit embodies a masculine principle. God's intention is for our spirit to have the headship of our soul. So conversely, our soul embodies a feminine principle; but once again, this is true *irrespective of our physical gender*. And wonder of all wonders, that which comes about through a loving relationship expressed in our being is why "sonship" also is not gender specific, as it is clearly stated in Galatians 3:26-28.

Both Jesus and the apostle Paul used the concept of marriage to instruct on many occasions. This is with good reason, for in the concept of marriage we have the reintegration into wholeness by that which was separate. The "marriage supper of the Lamb" is all about the reunification of man's mind, will, and emotions with God's Spirit. The soul is espoused to be wedded to the spirit now that her first husband (Adam) has died in Christ.

> So then, if while her husband is living she is joined to another man, she shall be called an adulteress; but if her husband dies, she is free from the law, so that she is not an adulteress though she is joined to another man. Therefore, my brethren, you also

50

were made to die to the Law through the body of Christ, so that you might be joined to another, to Him who was raised from the dead, in order that we might bear fruit for God. (Romans 7:3-4)

Having died to the law of adultery, our soul was free to be joined to the Lord. Then by receiving His incorruptible seed, our soul shall be saved in childbirth.

Therefore, putting aside all filthiness and all that remains of wickedness, in humility receive the word implanted, which is able to save your souls. (James 1:21)

Our soul would conceive of His word. Christ is now being formed in us through the travail of our earthly experience. And just as inevitable as is the outcome of physical gestation, our receptive soul shall "bear fruit for God" (bear a son unto God!)

Before she travailed, she brought forth; before her pain came, she was delivered of a male child. Who hath heard such a thing? Who hath seen such things? Shall the earth be made to bring forth in one day or shall a nation be born at once? for as soon as Zion travailed, she brought forth her children. "Shall I bring to the birth, and not cause to bring forth?" saith the LORD: "shall I cause to bring forth, and shut the womb?" saith thy God. (Isaiah 66:7-9)

For the perfect union of a *regenerated spirit* and a *transformed soul* will bring about the conception of the *man-child* (Revelation 12:1). This represents our *mature sonship* who when brought to the moment of birth (brought into manifestation) shall mean *the total redemption of the body*. Spirit, mind, and body — humanity integrated as a powerful new creation in the perfect image and likeness (character) of God. Immortality in Christ is truly an awesome inheritance!

Blessed be the God and Father of our Lord Jesus Christ, who in His great mercy has *begotten us anew* to an ever-living hope through the resurrection of Jesus Christ from the dead, to an inheritance imperishable, undefiled and unfading, which has been reserved in Heaven for you, whom God in His power is guarding through faith *for a salvation that even now stands ready for unveiling at the End of the Age.* (1 Peter 1:3-5; italics mine)

As the soul learns to yield to the Spirit in this affair of the heart, the spirit man is granted increasingly more freedom to express outwardly in an ever greater visible manifestation. This outward expression has been called "walking in the Spirit." As the submissive soul continually yields to the mind of the spirit and looks inward to Christ for her direction, she is transformed in the spirit of her mind (renewed). No longer leaning upon her own understanding, our soul happily finds her place at the feet of the mind of Christ.

Draw nigh to God, and He will draw nigh to you. (James 4:8)

Body, Spirit, Soul: A Foundation to Build Upon

It is my conviction that the main reason we struggle in our growth and strive with our maker is because we have so little understanding of our own makeup. For without a true foundational understanding of ourselves, the how and why of what we do seem to escape us. This, dear ones, leaves us somewhat unproductive—stymied in that foggy realm of fear and doubt.

Over the years, we have all listened to numerous sermons that have made an attempt to convey the concept of man having a *triune nature*. Personally, I have found most of these exposés lacking the depth necessary to set people free. Some of these "messages" have in fact been more harmful than helpful.

If we hope to cooperate with the plan of God for our lives and intelligently *lose our life* that we might find our soul preserved (aligned in the mind of Christ), then out of necessity, we are going to have to know something of the mechanics making us what we are.

Knowing full well that I have somewhat stretched my neck out here, I pray that our Father would use me to bring forth something fresh and alive that will minister to our need and help to unveil our understanding.

So now in the order that I believe is from the simple and obvious, to the more complex and subtle, I am hopeful that our Father may shed some newly anointed light on these subjects.

Father, we thank you for this in Jesus' name.

Body

I remember the days of old; I meditate on all thy works; I muse on the work of thy hands. (Psalm 143:5)

I believe all can agree that we have been given not only a beautiful but also wonderfully fascinating universe to explore and enjoy. Happily, we have also been given the perfect vehicle whereby we may, through experience, take in all the wonders of the world.

The human body is our interface with the three-dimensional world around us. It is through our bodies that we are affected by our environment. We have been endowed with five amazing senses. These senses *indiscriminately soak up and take in whatever information to which they happen to be exposed*. For example, sometimes my eyes suddenly see things that I would rather they not see. And just as unexpectedly, how easily the sublime beauty of a sunset can abruptly take my breath away. Again, our bodies are the interface through which we effect changes in the world. The body is the instrument whereby we make expression, whether it is in speech or in action, such as work, sports, dance, song, painting, sculpting, writing, etc.

Still, the body is perhaps not all that we take it to be. Undoubtedly, when you look in the mirror, you identify with the image that you see as being who you are; but this cannot possibly be because who you are is spirit and spirit cannot be seen. If the spirit is removed, the body, like a suit of clothes, will collapse in a heap, revealing its true nature. No, when you look in the mirror, you are looking at a "car," a vehicle that you will trade in some day for a new one — one that will not fade away. But truly, as the psalmist has said, "We are fearfully and wonderfully made."

However, there is another point that I believe needs to be made. Our body is the temple of the living God. And God does not and is not dwelling in an unholy temple! Some may be adhering to an immature idea that had its origin in Gnosticism. It is the idea that matter is inherently evil. Therefore, spirit is good, but the body is evil! Yet the prophet Isaiah received angelic testimony saying, "Holy, holy, holy is the *Lord* of hosts; the whole earth is full of His glory." Friends, even when we yield our members as instruments of unrighteousness, it does not alter the holy nature of God's glorious creation. The only thing this will do is dull our awareness of the sacred nature of our being and relationship.

54

Search your heart and cast down these imaginings when you find them. I assure you that — spirit, soul, and body — you are the holy offspring and ongoing creation of a Holy God! *So take off your shoes* (stop walking in your own strength, stop leaning on your own understanding) and thereby sanctify your ground in a holy understanding!

> For both He who sanctifies and those who are sanctified are all from one Father; for which reason He is not ashamed to call them brethren. (Hebrew 2:11)

Spirit

Here we will make the leap from the tangible to the intangible, from the physical aspects of our makeup to the nonphysical. *I believe there is much misunderstanding, if not outright confusion, concerning the difference between the spirit and the soul of man.* That being said, initially there are a few simple and direct statements that I am going to make in regard to the spirit that I believe are based in truth and not opinion. As such, they will stand up under the scrutiny of self-exploration. In other words, when you look into yourself, you will find these things to be so.

Your spirit is the timeless (ageless) essence that you are. It is the seat of your true identity. It is *who you actually are*. Not necessarily whom you have come to accept as yourself. Secondly, *your spirit is the knower, not the thinker*. It is that part of you that knows things, and it is fully aware that it knows that it knows! In addition to this natural capacity "you have an anointing from the Holy One, and you know all things" for "he that is joined unto the Lord is one spirit." Thirdly, your spirit witnesses everything you experience. *It is the watcher, the observer.* This aspect of our makeup literally has the capacity to stand beside our "self." Like a silent audience of one, it witnesses the drama of this life even while our mind, will, and emotions are animating our body in the drama. It is to this portion of ourselves that Jesus gave the injunction "watch and pray." Moreover, this aspect of ourselves enables us to walk circumspectly with an awareness not only of our own person but also of how our bearing is affecting those around us. This is our Spirit man.

For a fuller understanding of man's spirit, we need to realize that it has both a positional relationship in regard to Christ's once-for-all atonement and a personal relationship in regard to our soul's earthly experience in time. Each one of us has personally experienced the adversary as a dictatorial authority ruling over our *degenerate spirit* (Adam). This experience of Adam's lifeless spirit in relation to adversity is what made us slaves to sin. In Eden, the order of our makeup was twisted 180 degrees to serve adverse ends, namely the subjection of the soul to the pain of frustration and futility as declared in Romans 8:20-21.

Because our Loving Father uses all things after the counsel of His own will, this odyssey through pain and depravation has not only served to make us hungry for the Bread of Life, but in humility, it drove us home to our gracious Loving Father.

To understand the positional relationship of everyone's spirit, we need to look at what Christ accomplished at the cross.

> Knowing this, that our old man was crucified with Him, that the body of sin might be nullified, so that we no longer serve sin. (Romans 6:6)

> So also you count yourselves to be truly dead to sin, but alive to God in Christ Jesus our Lord. (Romans 6:11)

By Jesus declaring Himself the "Son of Man" (Son of Adam), He took on the persona of *the old man*. This identification was then sealed with a covenant that He made with humanity at the Last Supper. According to the terms of this covenant, Jesus would be fully identified with the warped nature we had inherited through our physical lineage. We in turn would be identified with the Lord of Glory and would inherit His divine nature from our spiritual Father.

Prior to this amazing covenant, Jesus only bore the testimony, "My food is to do the will of Him who sent Me and to accomplish His work." After making this covenant, our Lord began to experience a will that could stand in opposition to the perfect will of God. Finally, His identification with us was completed in the *Garden* of Gethsemane. There Jesus took on the curse that had been placed upon man's alienated consciousness in the *Garden* of Eden. Though *God was in Christ reconciling the world to Himself*, this curse would so darken our Lord's awareness of His Father's presence that He cried out from the cross "My God, my God, why have you forsaken me?"

> Christ redeemed us from the curse of the Law, having become a curse for us—for it is written, "cursed is everyone who hangs on a tree". (Galatians 3:13)

In other words, He identified with *the entire sin-ridden spirit of the Adamic race throughout time*; next, He carried this identification into *death*. On the cross, He destroyed it, never to rise again. This is one aspect of Jesus' title as the last Adam. In addition, this destruction is why you have a regenerated spirit.

Because Christianity, and the world in general, makes little or no distinction between the soul and the spirit, what I am about to say may be hard for some to currently grasp. I trust that our Father will alleviate this deficiency by the time we finish this book.

The instant humanity died on the cross (Romans 6:6), our Father reconstituted every man's spirit anew. Then, when Jesus rose by the power of God, so did the life of all men. The entire collective spirit life of humanity was raised up and seated (established) in the life of Christ. All reside in the heavenly city (a God-governed realm that lies outside of time and anyone's earthly experience).

> Even when we were dead in our transgressions, made us alive together with Christ (by grace you have been saved), and raised us up with Him, and seated us with Him in the heavenly places in Christ Jesus. (Ephesians 2:5-6)

> So then as through one transgression there resulted condemnation to all men, even so through one act of righteousness there resulted justification of life to all men. (Romans 5:18)

Seated in Christ, the incorruptible spirit life of every man eagerly desires to be united with his corresponding soul. Therefore, we need to add to our understanding that the Lord of glory *is currently the ruling authority* in man's *ascended spirit* (which for all mankind is forever unified in Christ). This is the positional relationship of every man's spirit to the efficacy of Christ's atonement.

Jesus — having declared for all time, "It is finished" — forever perfected man's spirit in Christ and has now set His sight upon man's wayward soul. But no man can come to Jesus unless the Father *draws* (literal Greek: *drags*) him.

> And the Lord was adding to their number day by day those who were being saved. (Acts 2:47)

Only those who have *been ordained to enter* into a *conscious relationship* with the Lord at their particular point in history have been called throughout this age. The rest of the blood-bought world is serving God's omniscient purpose in other ways — namely by providing a hostile-proving ground for the perfecting of a small cadre of *overcoming* sons.

> Now in a large house there are not only gold and silver vessels, but also vessels of wood and of earthenware, and some to honor and some to dishonor. (2 Timothy 2:20)

You see, it is only possible for a son to *"learn obedience"* in a contrary environment. Obedience may only be established and tested in an environment that allows for and promotes disobedience! Sonship's proving ground is a painful environment of suffering that tempts one at every turn to be disobedient to the call.

Self-preservation is a worldly custom that is universally accepted as wisdom in our present age. But this time-honored custom is the enemy of the cross. We will explore this more thoroughly in the chapters titled "The Will and the Emotions of the Soul."

> But turning around and seeing His disciples, He rebuked Peter and said, "Get behind Me, Satan; for you are not setting your mind on God's interests, but man's." And He summoned the crowd with His disciples, and said to them, "If anyone wishes to come after Me, he must deny himself, and take up his cross and follow Me." (Mark 8:33-34)

> Although He was a Son, He learned obedience from the things which He suffered. (Hebrews 5:8a)

Whoever is called into a conscious relationship under the lordship of Christ embarks on a process of sanctification whereby the soul is brought to the place where she becomes a perfect expression of the *mind of Christ* or has in truth "grown up into the head."

Philippians 2:5-8 instructs us to

> have this attitude in yourselves, which was also in Christ Jesus who, although He existed in the form of God, did not regard equality with God a thing to be grasped but emptied Himself, taking the form of a bond-servant, being made in the likeness of men. Being found in appearance as a man, He humbled Himself by becoming obedient to the point of death, even death on a cross.

Our soul is to grow in grace to the point where she will count it "all joy" to have this same attitude and mirror the self-sacrificing nature of her espoused husband. However, if you find the thought of that causing your flesh to cringe, it is because the cross we have been instructed to *take up* will forever remain foolishness to our perishing carnality. Pay it no mind; spirit beings are not debtors to the flesh!

Soul: Mind, Will, and Emotions

I could not begin to count the times I have heard the soul described as the mind, the will, and the emotions; and yes, it is so. Yet to put such a simplistic label on a subject of such import without exploring the implications of just what this means, I find to be morally negligent, or at the very least one-dimensional. By doing this, the most intricately complex and beautiful part of our humanity is virtually reduced to a meaningless cliché.

Our soul is a most difficult subject to write about because these three parts (the mind, will, and emotions) are so closely integrated and interrelated that there is not much division between them. It may even be that these divisions are not a concrete reality, but are an artificially imposed definition for the sake of discussion. Clearly, our feelings easily influence our thinking. The emotions that drive our feelings are affected by whether or not the demands (will) of the ego are met. I would ask the reader to keep these interrelationships (entanglements) in mind as we explore this aspect of our humanity. I trust that our Father will continue to show even more that lies between and beyond my words.

The Mind of the Soul

What a tangled web we weave, when first we practice to deceive. (Sir Walter Scott)

My, my, my, what a tangled mess I found my mind in when shortly after an encounter with the King of Glory I began to look within. I've heard it said, "Man wants inward understanding, and yet he will not look within." Truthfully, I think I would have run away, never to look back, were it not for the gentle and persistent urgings of my Savior saying, "It'll be all right, and it will be worth it. Fear not, I am with you, my child. I will help you." Faithfully He has as each new twist and turn of my thoughts and memory were exposed in His light. I was transfixed in the wonder of His liberating fire as it freed me from various entanglements of emotion and illusory belief systems.

Self-deception is highly insidious because he who is deceived is the very last one to know it. The mind, being conditioned by what it thinks it knows, simply prevents one from seeing anything that lies outside of its preconceived notions and/or strongly held opinions. Our own mind can easily become an idol. "Having eyes they see not and ears they hear not." The happy prisoner of a mind like this can only see to the limits of their self-imposed box, but for them it appears to be the extent of what can be known.

Albert Einstein quite aptly said, "It is the theory that decides what can be observed."

Our mind can be likened to just so much soft clay. Because like clay, it retains impressions that have been pressed upon it—things like our experiences and the emotions we have associated with each experience. Herein lies the rub. Our mind, will, and emotions, under the dictates of our domineering first husband Adam, have taken a set, a *mind-set* if you will. In fact, many mind-sets about all of the things it has been exposed to in its "infinitely grand" experience. The mind will unconsciously take a set whenever it accepts what it perceives as reality. (Whether it actually is or not is of little or no consequence.) The memories of our perceptions are literally pressed between the pages of our minds. *Our experiences or our relationship to our memories, with their emotional attachments (baggage), is part of what we have come to identify as being who we are.*

May the Lord deliver us from our identification with our history! Regarding this, there is a great deal of freedom to be found when we come to the place where we can say, in all humility, "Of my own self I can know nothing." We gain freedom whenever we become comfortable with the realization that we are not qualified to form opinions. Because from this point on, we will not trust our own opinion, neither will we take our mind in an overly serious manner. It is through this change of heart that we shall begin to breathe a sigh of relief.

Through a willingness to no longer lean upon our own understanding, we provide the necessary *S-P-A-C-I-O-U-S-N-E-S-S* for the mind of Christ to manifest. Sharing His mind, we are empowered to deal with the world and ourselves differently. By the simple provision of room for the King, love will have made an entrance into all of our affairs.

> Father, I allow you to show me who I actually am. In your great mercy, show me how to think and deal with whom I have erroneously come to believe myself to be. Help me to cast down these distorted images and come to see myself as only you would have me see. Amen.

The renewed mind is a powerful and highly disciplined tool, but the unrenewed mind is as the run-amuck, self-absorbed fool.

All believers are in a process of renewal, whether we are conscious of His dealings with us or not! While it is true that some areas of our thinking have currently been set in order, other areas are yet to be addressed. The real beauty of this is it really is not our job to fix ourselves. Our Redeemer has a purpose and plan that incorporates a custom-tailored agenda to personally deal with every individual. He is in full control of our circumstances at all times. Even those times having the appearance of being wildly out of control. It is in *trying times* such as this that I have found the Lord showing me some previously hidden shortcoming in my thinking. His grace exposing some skewed value judgment, or something that the circumstances brought to the forefront of my awareness, there to be dealt with in the glorious light of His wisdom and love.

You see, a man can only turn from (repent of) that which he can clearly see in himself. Whenever a man, *whose heart has been captured* by the lover of his soul, sees something amiss in his personality, that man will not only turn from it immediately; but he will do so effortlessly and in the perfect peace of love—without condemnation!

There is only one source of *love* in this universe—God! Apart from a healthy connection to this source, humanity has a mere empty concept! God's love is continually shed abroad in our hearts by the Holy Spirit. Connected to our source, it makes it possible to fulfill the following scripture.

When Jesus was asked,

> "Teacher, which is the greatest commandment in the Law?" He answered, "Thou shalt *love* the lord thy *God*, with thy *whole heart*, thy *whole soul*, thy *whole mind*. This is the greatest and foremost commandment. And the second is similar to it: Thou shalt *love* thy fellow *man* as much *as thyself*. The whole of the Law and the Prophets is summed up in these two Commandments." (Matthew 22:36-40; italics mine)

Seeing that this is the first and foremost commandment, a true understanding of the law and its prophets is hinged upon this central pivot of loving *God, thyself,* and *man*. It then becomes imperative that we get our point of origin right, or everything else is vanity! The Kingdom of God and the royal law of life in Christ work purely in love!

We can only love God in wholeness! With a double or divided heart (well of emotions), divided soul (will), or divided mind (intellect), we cannot actually love God. While in a divided state, we may easily fool ourselves about loving Him. The truth is, because of this division, we are not actually free to love God. This is why we are told in James 4:8 to *cleanse our hands* (the instruments of the will) and to *purify our hearts, we that are double-minded*. Ultimately it is our heart's conflicting emotions that drives our conflicted thinking. All of us, 100 percent, need work in this area! However, if you are one who thinks that he has a pretty good grip on things, you are probably the one who needs a deeper work than the man who cries in all humility, "Be merciful to me, a sinner."

> If we say that we have no sin, we are deceiving ourselves and the truth is not in us. (1 John 1:8)

While this particular scripture might be highly instructive to some, most are painfully aware that our mind, will, and emotions are in dire need of some major spring-cleaning! Because the sheer volume of the accumulated conflict easily overwhelms us, we have instead become much more accustomed to simply closing the doors on the messy museum of the mind! Yet everyone declares his desire to see God and be done with this double-minded turmoil!

Blessed are the pure in heart, for they shall see God. (Matthew 5:8)

Levels of Awareness

Before we enlist the agency of our helper, the Holy Spirit, in the daunting cleanup operation of the renovation of the mind, perhaps it would be good to take a tour through its structure. We are now going to explore a slightly different aspect of man having a *triune nature*.

There are *three distinct levels of awareness* within the mind of man: the *conscious*, the *preconscious*, and the *subconscious*. The *conscious awareness* is that faculty which enables us to focus our attention on whatever task is at hand and, in turn, allows us to bring our will to bear on that particular issue. Part of what enables us to accomplish this feat of focused attention is our preconscious awareness.

I believe the best way to convey the nature of our preconscious awareness is in a demonstration. While you are reading this, you are aware of many things that are not immediately apparent. For instance, you are aware of whether you find the current temperature comfortable. You are aware of whether you have adequate light for reading. You are aware of whether there is any noise in the room or perhaps filtering in from the outside. If there are others in the vicinity, you may be aware of their activities and perhaps even their mood.

As I have brought your attention to each of these things, they were raised from the preconscious to conscious awareness when the focus of your attention was redirected. Much of our mind runs on autopilot, and this is a tremendous blessing for it frees us to concentrate. The third area of our awareness is the subconscious, and it could be considered both a blessing and a curse (though actually, in truth, it is amoral).

> My son, pay attention to my words; stretch your ear to what I say; let them not depart from your eyes; keep them in the center of your heart; for they are life to those who find them, and healing to all his flesh. Keep your heart with all diligence, for out of it are the issues of life. Turn away from you the crooked mouth, and put perverse lips far from you. Let your eyes look straight ahead, and let your eyelids look straight before you. (Proverbs 4:20-25)

* Pay attention to my words . . . keep them in the center of your *heart*.
* Keep your *heart* with all diligence for out of it are the issues of life.

* Out of the abundance of the *heart* the mouth speaks.
* A good man, *out of the good treasure of the heart,* bringeth forth good things; and an evil man, *out of the evil treasure,* bringeth forth evil things.

When the Bible speaks about the *heart,* it is not talking about the marvelous blood pump that beats in our chest. It is being descriptive; as in nature, the heartwood of a tree is the very core of the tree. The *heart* of man is the core or deepest part of his mind that in modern terms has been called the subconscious.

Our Treasure Trove

The subconscious mind is much like a black hole; things go in but they don't come out. Well, at least *not in ways we are consciously aware*, until after the fact. Hence, this part of the mind is seemingly shrouded in a certain amount of mystery. We have a tendency to shroud things in mystery that our conscious mind cannot quite quantify, and then pin down as a reference point.

The subconscious mind can be looked at like a vast library, a colossal depository more complex than you are able to easily imagine. So if I may paint for us a picture:

> Contained in our heart's storehouse of treasure are every experience we have ever had, every emotion we have ever felt, every word we've ever spoken, every sight our eyes have ever taken in. Included is every thought and imagination we've ever entertained — a memory of all the sights, smells, and sounds of our day-to-day interactions with our culture. Contained therein is a complete record of every nuance of our lives: *all attitudes, resentments, fears, faiths, and the real roots of our belief systems.*

Before I give the impression that the subconscious mind is merely a sack into which all things are dumped, there are some aspects of this part of our makeup that needs to be brought out. Have you ever noticed you can go to sleep at night with some problem or unresolved issue only to awaken in the morning with the solution?

> I will bless the Lord who has counseled me; Indeed, my mind instructs me in the night. (Psalm 16:7)

The subconscious part of our mind never sleeps. While our conscious and preconscious awareness shuts down for the night, the subconscious utilizes its vast resources and continues to work on solutions to whatever issues are paramount. Additionally, our experience of intuition is the result of information welling up from our subconscious awareness. For instance, upon meeting someone for the first time, our subconscious awareness is very busy sizing up the individual. Subconsciously, we pick up on tonal inflections of voice and body language and, most likely, are reading a host of other cues for which we have no name. All of this information then automatically gets placed in a file on this person. This is why a person's first impression upon the clay of our mind is so important.

Issues of Life and Death

By far, the greatest part of our mental activity takes place in the subconscious. Modern researchers have estimated that depending upon the individual, the subconscious activity of our electrochemical biocomputer processes information on the amazing order of five hundred thousand to one million times more efficiently than our conscious, rational mind.

The conscious mind reasons *inductively*. Gathering facts, it linearly reasons upward toward a conclusion based upon those facts. Whereas, the subconscious mind reasons *deductively*; intuitively the subconscious begins with a conclusion. Then much like a multitasking Sherlock Holmes proceeds to fill in the missing pieces until the entire picture is apprehended. It is this capacity that enables the subconscious mind (heart) to operate in perfect faith. Essentially, the subconscious finishes its understanding and then begins to support it. For instance, when the implications of God's Word concerning the incorruptibility of His implanted seed settled down into the *heart of my soul* (subconscious mind), it obliterated all doubt and fear about not being preserved blameless at His appearing. For an incorruptible seed must, by its very nature, bring forth a perfect crop unto harvest.

> In humility receive the word implanted, which is able to save your souls. (James 1:21)

This same capacity of our subconscious can be turned inside out, and the results of this are highly irrational fears based largely on imaginings. Fear is actually faith in the negative! The reason that this is so powerful is that the subconscious does not have the capacity to *differentiate* between what is real and what is imaginary. Rather it accepts both without question as being equally valid. Much like a small child accepts without question his or her reality of Santa Claus or the boogeyman. Their perfect faith brings forth perfect trust, and they enter into creative belief. Our mind never lost this awesome capacity; the only question for us: is it being utilized as an asset or a liability?

> And having called forward a little child, Jesus set him in their midst. And He said, "Truly I say to you, unless you convert and become as the little children, not at all can you enter into the kingdom of Heaven.

Then whoever will humble himself as this little child, this one is the greater in the kingdom of Heaven. And whoever will receive one such little child in My name receives Me." (Matthew 18:2-5)

Imagine a five-year-old with almost unlimited creative and destructive potential, and you will begin to get the picture why our subconscious mind (heart) needs a transformation. Now receive this beautiful but somewhat-wounded child in Jesus' name, and in the power of His love, your subconscious awareness (heart) will begin to heal unto wholeness.

GIGO

Programmers in the software industry have come up with this little gem, GIGO, which stands for "garbage in, garbage out." The thought being whatever errors or mistakes a programmer makes in writing, the software's code will later show up as glitches, bugs, or errata of one form or another. The subconscious mind has much in common with this principle. We should be aware that we are, to a large extent, being force-fed much garbage by our culture—religion, politics, advertising, the movie industry, video games, and the like. Even we, at times without thinking, participate in destructive things like gossip and backbiting, which strongly influence how we perceive one another. All of these environmental contaminations poison our minds and hearts and defile our relationship with God, self, and neighbor.

So what are we to do about all of this? Well, contained within the word of God is clear instruction that constitutes a very effective antidote for the toxic nature of our age. And we would do well to slowly meditate upon the implications of each word in the following passage:

> Finally, brethren, whatever is true, whatever wins respect, whatever is just, whatever is pure, whatever is lovable, whatever is of good repute—if there is any virtue or anything deemed worthy of praise—cherish the thought of these things. (Philippians 4:8)

I AM CHRIST WITHIN

* I AM healthy, hopeful, and optimistic.
* I AM vigorous, relaxed, and accepted.
* I AM trusting, participative, and open-minded.
* I AM sensitive, creative, and purposeful.
* I AM capable, resourceful, and wise.
* I AM generous, ethical, and loveable.
* I AM loyal, considerate, and trustworthy.
* I AM genuine, tender, and caring.
* I AM alert, aware, and responsible.
* I AM genuinely concerned about others.

71

If we focus upon the anointing,
we will come to cherish who we are;
with every poison swallowed by an ocean of love,
we shall realize who we are!

As we willingly align in the *truth*, because we have come to see it as the only wise *way* to walk, our eye will become singularly fixed on things above. Our whole body will be filled with light, and our *life* will begin to resonate with the heart and mind of God. *Complete victory* over the world, the flesh, and the devil is not only possible; it is the very purpose for our life in Christ.

To the praise of His glory, the Lord shall have a people that will *walk* as a perfect expression of His total victory. No doubt, this will be to the utter consternation of the scoffers and naysayers as they gnash their teeth in the realization of how they have been robbed by their favorite religious notions!

> And they overcame him because of the blood of the Lamb, and because of the Word of their testimony. And they did not love their soul even until death. (Revelation 12:11)

*   "If any man will come after me let him take up his cross and follow me."
*   "And they did not love their soul even until death."

Have you ever noticed the place that *Jesus crucified* His likeness of sinful *flesh* is called Golgotha and that it means "the place of the skull"? (Remember that He said, "No man takes my life. I have been given power to lay it down and take it up again.")

> I plead with you therefore, brethren, by the compassions of God, to present all your faculties to Him as a living and holy sacrifice acceptable to Him. This with you will be an act of reasonable worship. (Romans 12:1; Weymouth New Testament)

The holy sacrifice spoken of here is all about our minds, friends. We also have the power to lay down our life and preserve it — *take it up again* to life eternal! For . . . *every sacrifice shall be salted with salt* (preserved). Once again, allow me to remind us, this is about the mind's attitude of utter submission!

Past, Present, Future

At the same time *two robbers* were crucified with Him, one at His right hand and the other at His left. (Matthew 27:38; italics mine)

Insults of the same kind were heaped on Him even by the *robbers* who were being crucified with Him. (Matthew 27:44; italics mine)

Now one of the criminals who had been crucified insulted Him, saying, "Are not you the Christ? Save yourself and us." But the other, answering, reproved him. (Luke 23:39-40)

And he said, "Jesus, remember me when you come in your Kingdom." "I tell you in solemn truth," replied Jesus, "that this very day you shall be with me in Paradise." (Luke 23:42-43)

If I may brush aside the bony pharisaical finger pointing that consigns one of these poor fellows to "hell" and one to "heaven", let us look anew at the essence of what was being presented here.

Salvation is lifted up between *two robbers*, one on His right and one on His left. Both of these men are suffering in a highly agitated state. In an incoherent outcry of pain, both are verbally striking out and hurling insults along with the crowd. Suddenly, one of the robbers, through the fog of all this *pain*, begins to remember the man who fed five thousand, the man who calmed the sea, who cleansed lepers and raised the dead. He begins to spy a hope and thinks to himself: Since you are obviously the man who *has been* and *has done* all of these marvelous things in the *past*, you can save us! Therefore he cried out, "Are not you the Christ? Save yourself and us." This man was desperately clinging to the life he had known. The other more self-centered robber spied a different hope and so reproved the former and said, "Jesus, remember me when you come in your kingdom." The implication being that since you are obviously the man of importance you are going to be in the *future*, remember me, the one who had the good sense to see that you were dying unjustly! (Perhaps, religious pride that he wasn't made like this other sinner?) This man was clinging to a life that his mind was projecting.

73

Frankly Jesus said to them both, "I tell you in solemn truth, that *this very day* [presently], you shall be with me in Paradise."

Our mind has two robbers, and they are both capable of stealing not only our peace and rest but also our opportunities for growth. By not releasing our pain and the involvement with our personal *past* and/or by projecting a vicarious life into an imagined *future*, the self-preserving tactics of the carnal mind rob us blind. The only way that we can lay down our life as a living sacrifice is to stay centered in the *present*! Presently, "if you hear his voice, do not harden your heart." The realization of our salvation is only to be found through a presence of mind in the nitty-gritty, *mean and nasty* here and now. *That was not factually a true statement!*

In truth, the present moment can be neither "good" nor "bad; it just is. *The present should be honored and accepted for whatever it is in a trusting attitude of full submission to our sovereign Father.* Whether or not the present moment satisfies our preferences is immaterial.

> This is the day which the Lord has made; Let us rejoice and be glad in it. (Psalm 118:24)

If we allow our mind to live in evaluation and label the present, we will be tempted to escape into the memories of the past or entertain imaginations of the future. And thus, like Esau of old, we unwittingly trade our birthright for a warm pot of illusion!

At this point, you may want to buckle your spiritual seat belt because the ride through the chapters "The Will of the Soul" and "The Emotions of the Soul" may get a little bumpy at times.

The Will of the Soul

I find it very telling that we had to be told the carnal mind is enmity with God. Furthermore, that it cannot submit itself to God. I pray that the blindness this indicates is so obvious that you can read between the lines here!

It is crucially important that we gain a revelation of the mind that has been our lifelong companion! For without gaining a clear revelation, we shall continue to accept this betrayer as a trusted friend. We need to realize that there is not a single aspect of this mind that is not opposed to everything that is called God! While some of this opposition is clearly visible to us, by and large, the majority of it is veiled from our view. Interestingly, the more religious a person becomes, the more hidden the opposition becomes. But whether it is visible or hidden, all of the opposition is inextricably linked to the will.

> For I know that nothing good dwells in me, that is, in my flesh; for the willing is present in me, but the doing of the good is not. (Romans 7:18)

Before we proceed, I need to define some terms in the way that I mean them and, therefore, will be using them.

1. Willful: An unyielding state of being, whereby an independent self or self-sufficient person thinks he/she determines everything—the ego's illusion of freewill.

2. Willing: A compliant state of being that merely honors everything being determined through the action of an outside agency—Almighty God.

Again, the carnal mind is enmity with God! Even on its best-est day or good-est behavior—while putting on its God-praisin', hallelujah-shoutin', Sunday-go-to-meetin' best—it is still 100 percent Antichrist. Organized religion for thousands of years has been trying to overcome evil with a carnal understanding of what is good, only to discover in the final analysis that they both hang from the same tree. The word *Antichrist* does not simply mean, as most would think, something easily distinguishable as being opposite to Christ. *Anti* in this particular case means "instead of, or counterfeit." (Strong's G473). *It looks entirely acceptable, yet is not*!

Our concerted efforts to make our beastly mind more presentable will definitely make us more socially acceptable. Although this inevitably results in some degree of what is called self-righteousness. Convincing as this counterfeit robe of righteousness is, it only fools us into believing our soul is "glory bound." For God declares, "Our righteous deeds are like a filthy garment."

> But when the king came in to look over the dinner guests, he saw a man there who was not dressed in wedding clothes, and he said to him, "Friend, how did you come in here without wedding clothes?" And the man was speechless. "Then the king said to the servants, "Bind him hand and foot, and throw him into the outer darkness; in that place there will be weeping and gnashing of teeth." (Matthew 22:11-13)

> Here is wisdom. Let him who has understanding calculate the number of the beast, for the number is that of a man; and his number is six hundred and sixty-six. (Revelation 13:18)

Oh my, what an amazing and perfectly wonderful trap has been set for the beastly carnal mind! What better way could there be than to give the willful egoic mind a *riddle* to challenge and engage it, and thereby keep it from returning and being healed? Our Father is a master craftsman of futility!

I have received some criticism for implying that our Father would intentionally frustrate any soul, so let us see what Father's word actually has to say on the subject.

> And I saw every work of God, I concluded that man cannot discover the work which has been done under the sun. Even though man should seek laboriously, he will not discover; and though the wise man should say, "I know," he cannot discover. (Ecclesiastes 8:17)

> For the creation was subjected to futility, not willingly, but because of Him who subjected it, in hope. (Romans 8:20)

In the garden, man made a willful choice to embrace a system of *knowledge* separate and apart from the wisdom of God. This resulted in the creation of a hideous abstraction known as the carnal mind. This mind is the lowest form of animal life on this planet! The nature of every other form effortlessly fulfills its God-given purpose!

We must come to realize that this is our enemy incarnate! But then again, great warriors are made by great enemies. Those who overcome this sly clandestine foe shall truly reign as kings in this universe!

The salvation of our soul will never be found through engaging the very mind from which we need salvation! *This approach will not work* even when religiously attempted *in the name of Jesus*!

> We were pregnant, we writhed in labor, we gave birth, as it seems, only to wind. We could not accomplish deliverance for the earth, nor were inhabitants of the world born. (Isaiah 26:18)

Our carnal mind was the booby prize created out of the willful rebellious act of a creative being! *Awdawm's* finest work was the adulterous procreation of the ego-driven mind that we have all come to know, love, and blindly defend to our last gasp! When Eve received the serpent's word into her consciousness, his word (seed) conceived his thoughts in her mind. This psychological rape of Eve's innocent mind would result in the conception of his body of opposing thought, the ego-self. Eve would then see the tree as acceptable and her ego-self in wont of it. It was the fruit of the serpent — his progeny, the newly formed ego in Eve that would drive her to willfully eat the fruit of rebellion.

> When the woman saw that the tree was good for food, and that it was a delight to the eyes, and that the tree was desirable to make one wise, she took from its fruit and ate; and she gave also to her husband with her, and he ate. (Genesis 3:6)

> And I will put enmity between you and the woman, And between your seed and her seed; He shall bruise you on the head, and you shall bruise him on the heel. (Genesis 3:15)

This miscreant of mind (the serpent's seed) has been handed down to us as our Adamic heritage. The true salvation of our soul (our soul's true healing) can only be found by *becoming willing* to forsake that heritage! Please read again my definition of *willing*, and you will discover that there is no forsaking for you to do. In the humility of our helplessness, we are merely occupying a space of agreement that will allow for it to happen.

77

Even the *choice* to be "willing" cannot be one of our *conscious* intellect, but rather must be a profound change of heart! This type of gut-level repentance is never born from anything but abject *brokenness*. Brokenness is the result of utter frustration to the point of conceding defeat and thereby retiring our will!

Because the carnal mind took on all the devious subtlety of the beastly serpent that spawned its rebellion, it will likely try to convince you that your best course of action now is to willfully choose to be willing!

This is a self-preserving tactic of carnality. It is an endless chasing of our tail that goes nowhere, but it does burn time and will even further frustrate you! However, this only brings us back to the required humility of brokenness for true willingness to manifest.

Yes, God will most assuredly frustrate our mind, will, and emotions! Nevertheless, because of what it accomplishes, it is a win-win situation for the both of us! This is the enigmatic meaning behind the statement: "He subjected it to futility in hope."

To sum this up as plainly as possible, *666* is merely *the beastly carnal number of man.* It is the biblical number designating the Adamic race in a fallen condition! Man's collective ego struggling in this willful system of knowledge is the spirit of Antichrist! For the enmity of carnality masquerades in the struggle between good and evil! Oh, how easily we justify our evil in the cause of good! This is what Isaiah saw when he declared, "I am undone!"

Two Faces of the Same System

The secular and the sacred present to us two faces of the same system. I have often felt that the psychologists have had a field day toying with an endless parade of ideas all to see who could get the best handle on man's problem. Truthfully, some of their observations are quite remarkable. Yet those of a secular bent remain clueless as to what the answer is. On the other hand, the religionists have immaturely toyed with seeing who could get the best grip on the answer. These remain largely ignorant of the nature of man's dilemma.

All religions are a contrivance of the natural ego-driven mind that rules mankind. The differences seen in the various religions of the world all stem from the rational machinations of the mind of man.

Each culture, in attempting to get a grip on the intangible nature of the one and only deity, has in turn come up with their own ethnic recipe. Please, don't get me wrong here. Religion has served our Father's purposes perfectly. The mind not governed by the spirit of truth is in need of some outward form of governance.

Religion has served to moderate the world's tendency to spin out of control into anarchy and total chaos. It has put on the brakes just enough for culture and secular government to flourish in the human experience.

Actually, *God* transcends all religion and is seeking to reveal *a dynamic living relationship with all of mankind*. Ironically, the largest impediment to this revelation is religion itself. Religion is essentially an egocentric intellectual pursuit. This pursuit will never be the basis upon which God relates to the spiritual nature of man.

Man's religious mind essentially sits on the sidelines, and in his aloof independence, he analyzes God. Very much like a frog pinned down in a biology class, he dissects God while maintaining his illusion of isolation and separateness. Next, he assembles his findings into a system known as theology. Through the blindness of theology, we do much violence to our potential relationship with our Father! This is because theology leads us to believe that we know something, when in fact we know nothing as we ought to know!

Very few people realize how violent an act the forming of opinion is. While this type of worldly wisdom may appear to serve us in our daily affairs, it is wholly inadequate when it comes to telling us who God is or who we are in Christ. The Mind of Christ does not form opinions. It has no need to decide what is or is not true.

The Christ Mind is an ongoing expression of our Father's manifold wisdom! It intimately knows the truth of all things. The forming of opinion is exclusively an activity of the carnal mind. Whether or not we realize it, the mind that employs these tactics to understand God is attempting to know something about God apart from a living connection with the wisdom of God.

If I may be allowed to point out, there is something *intrinsically wrong* with the finite mind attempting to define the limits of an infinite God. Regarding this, it is most unfortunate that man's efforts appear to succeed; for in every improved definition, a new religion, sect, or denomination is born.

Including Christianity, every religion on the face of this planet has reverse-engineered God using the only reference point that man has devised. This untrustworthy reference is what he thinks he knows of himself. After all, were we not created in His image? By this, we have repeatedly created a God in our own flawed image. "Professing to be wise, they became fools and exchanged the glory of the incorruptible God for an image in the form of corruptible man."

Dear reader, take a moment to reflect on the light of God. How it has given pause to your understanding. In what ways it has challenged you. How it is apparently transforming your awareness, though you may not even know how. I ask you to take the time to do this, that you might find reason to do what I now ask. I am about to challenge your thinking again and touch some things that you are very likely to hold sacred. To avoid any automatic defensiveness (a distraction that only hinders), I ask that you even further suspend judgment until God's light dawns.

A Carnal Masterpiece: The First Denomination

The rise of the religious arm of Babylon was born in the simple act of exchanging a verb for noun. *Webster's Dictionary* defines denomination as:

Denomination, noun.

1. The act of naming.
2. A name or appellation; a vocal sound, customarily used to express a thing or a quality, in discourse; as, all men fall under the denomination of sinners; actions fall under the denomination of good or bad.
3. A class, society or collection of individuals, called by the same name; as a denomination of Christians.

Jesus never came to establish any form of religion! He came to accomplish two things. The first was to reveal the truly loving character and provision of our Father through Immanuel — God with us. God walking in union with the physicality of mankind! This is why *Jesus* constantly referred to himself as "the son of man!" He is not ashamed to call us brethren!

The second was that *Jesus* came to show *us how to walk* (i.e., the way) in continual conscious union with our Father. You see, it is *we* who *are our Father's house.* We are *His* many dwelling places (temple) walking this earth!

In My *Father's house* are many dwelling places; if it were not so, I would have told you; for I go to prepare a place for you. If I go and prepare a place for you, I will come again and receive you to Myself, that where I am, there you may be also. (John 14:2-3; italics mine)

Parabolic translation:

If I go away, I will, through my atoning work, prepare your heart to receive me as the *Holy Spirit,* that where I am, in union with our Father, there your conscious awareness may be also!

"For this reason, rejoice, O heavens and you who dwell in them". Those who dwell with their *head* in the *heavens* and their feet upon the earth will walk above the course of this world!

The vibrant church of the living God is and always was to have been the normal everyday manifestation of the way to walk in union with our Father!

It was the opposition inherent in the natural mind of the Jews and the pagans that would be first to hang a carnal label upon those who were "walking in the way!" It was at Antioch that the first denomination was unwittingly born.

I acknowledge that this may be a little too esoteric for some to see easily. Therefore, let us explore a more in-depth explanation to bring our understanding into focus.

It is in the nature of the willful carnal mind to place a value on all things. Our fleshly mind does this compulsively so the ego can feel safe and comfortable within the confines of its established reference points. In fact, if the ego ever stopped its incessant evaluating, its house of opinion cards would come crashing down; and it would be exposed for the lie that it is. Therefore, it is endlessly weighing and assigning value as it sees fit in regard to quantity or quality. It must behave in this manner in order to place what it believes to be an appropriate label.

Because of the distortion that is inherent in our fleshly perceptions, the carnal mind cannot touch the things of God without defiling them. So essentially, all that the adversary had to do to delay his imminent imprisonment was tempt and tease the carnal mind into changing the *how* (of walking in the way) into a *what* (Christian).

The subtle misdirection of consciousness that was the result of this distortion was enough to cause the church to wander forty jubilees (two thousand years) in the wilderness! Without this misdirection, the Dark Ages would never have been possible.

In the simple attachment of the label "Christian," a previously nondescript yet *all-inclusive "walk" in the Spirit* would instantly become an exclusive sect. Prior to hanging a label on God's "awakened" children, the only way you could recognize them was by witnessing the fruit of the Spirit in their demeanor.

This manner of recognition was hardly useful for a reference point because the ego, being a fiction itself, "lives" not in the three-dimensional world but in the imagination of the carnal mind.

One moment, man was experiencing an open and freely expanding presence because God had drawn a love circle around the whole world. In the next, otherwise godly men had unwittingly shrunken the circle around a fraction of the populace that it segregated when they accepted the new label "Christian"!

In time, this embryonic elitism would manifest itself visibly. Most notably, in the wonderfully creative thinking, "you've got to be in our club or you're going to be eternally tormented"! For God so loved the church that He gave His only begotten Son? Everyone else He left behind! Religion will forever remain content to keep its monetary power base on the cutting edge of ignorance!

The spiritually dead *religion of Christianity* would be the inevitable result of this exclusivity and would eventually give rise to a religious *Mother of Harlots*. From the perversions of a Roman mother, an endless stream of denominations and splinter groups would eventually descend!

By their cherished distinctives, each descendant would become increasingly isolated and insulated from one another and the world at large. Thirty-one thousand flavors of growing confusion—Babylon prepackaged in boxes, "ticky-tacky boxes all in a row"! An ineffectual and divided house that *cannot* stand would be the ultimate result of the natural mind perverting the concept carried by the verb *walk* into the noun *Christian*.

It has been said by some that the word *Christian* means "*little* Christ," while others have said that it means "*like* Christ." Both of these concepts are false! In fact, they are an absolute lie because they are not even possible. There is only one Christ, and we are all members in particular of that *one*!

> There is one body and one Spirit, just as also you were called in one hope of your calling; one Lord, one faith, one baptism, one God and Father of all who is over all and through all and in all. (Ephesians 4:4-6)

Both concepts for this ridiculous *label* imply a separation that simply does not exist! The only "*little* Christ" or "*like* Christ" there can possibly be is *Antichrist*!

By the independent carnal willfulness of the ego, humanity had carried their alienated consciousness right over into their New Testament experience with God! Christianity, while believing itself to have escaped the world's deception, is by its very name the finest example of it!

My purpose is not to depress anyone but to show how hidden opposition inherent in the willfulness of our carnality has propelled our understanding into "dire straits." These are treacherous waters of ignorance! The natural mind is so blind to its own blindness!

To bring things into a balanced perspective, we need to remember the church age is under a Pentecostal anointing. This measured anointing does not have the power to perfect a spotless bride. Even a cursory reading of the letters to the churches reveals the meaning of the two loaves (two thousand years) that were baked with leaven. These loaves were presented as a wave offering before the Lord on the day of Pentecost.

The perfecting of the bride will take nothing less than the fiery dispensation of the Age of Tabernacles. We are currently entering this age when the fullness of His presence will be revealed in His remnant sons!

> For the anxious longing of the creation waits eagerly for the revealing of the sons of God. (Romans 8:19)

I can't seem to see the forest. There's all these trees in the way!

Two Minds, Two Trees

Sometimes, to better understand where we are, it is helpful to revisit where we have been. With a few simple keystrokes, we find ourselves standing in the midst of the Garden of Eden. To the right of us is the Tree of Life, and to our immediate left is the Tree of Knowledge of Good and Evil. Oh, the choices, choices, choices. To partake of either tree "is to draw our sustenance from that source."

When I eat from the Tree of Life, I find life effortlessly springing forth from my being. I have peace like a river flowing forth to me and out from me to the world. My life simply unfolds before me without taking any more thought than breathing. I am free and at home in the quiet dignity of my being. I am at one with my maker. I am continually aware of His mind and will in all things. I live in a superabounding world with endless supply, for my Daddy owns it all, and He in every way has become my all in all.

> Before going further, allow me to interject this: The promises to the overcomers are not just some "pie in the sky." They are present realities that shall have their ultimate fulfillment in the fullness of time. We need these divine enablements and ennoblements *now in this life*, while the battle rages. So the question is, *Are we actively aligning with our Father's process of overcoming worldly influence, the fleshly nature, and the deceptive spirit of condemnation?*

Now back to our trees. When I eat from the all-too-familiar Tree of Knowledge of Good and Evil (death on a stick), immediately my rational, reasoning mind springs into action. It has been put to task, figuring out just what is good and what is evil. In addition to what, just how evil and how good is it? Is there something better? Endlessly weighing and then assigning value, so I can label and categorize, thus putting my ducks in a row. All of this is needful to make informed decisions. These things are so terribly important, oh, don't you know!? How else is a body to live than by his own wit and wile? And by the way, I'm better at it than you are bucko! Y'er not about to be gittin' one up on me!

The Jews persecuted Jesus for *making a man whole* on the Sabbath, and Jesus answered them (in a very peculiar way for a Hebrew) saying, "My Father is working until now, and I, Myself, am working" (John 5:17). No matter how you slice it, this is an extraordinary statement because in the context that it was said, it placed us squarely in the sixth day of creation! (This would not be the only instance that our Lord would violate our notions of time.) Oh, the choices, choices, choices.

> Giving thanks to the Father, who has qualified us to share in the inheritance of the saints in Light. For He rescued us from the domain of darkness, and transferred us to the kingdom of His beloved Son. (Colossians 1:12-13)

It is through our gracious birth from above that we were born as subjects in His illuminated *kingdom*. However, the literal meaning of the word *kingdom* is "the dominion of the king." It is the realm over which a king sovereignly rules by right and authority.

> Why do you call Me, "Lord, Lord," and do not do what I say? Everyone who comes to Me and hears My words and acts on them, I will show you whom he is like: he is like a man building a house, who dug deep and laid a foundation on the rock; and when a flood occurred, the torrent burst against that house and could not shake it, because it had been well built. But the one, who has heard and has not acted accordingly, is like a man who built a house on the ground without any foundation; and the torrent burst against it and immediately it collapsed, and the ruin of that house was great. (Luke 6:46-49)

The reason we frequently find ourselves not doing what He says is because someone is still usurping His rightful authority as king. That someone is willfully choosing to sit upon the throne within our temple. This usurper is Antichrist. You may be much better acquainted with him under the title of self. Initially, most people find the idea of that so shocking that they recoil and simply reject it out of hand. Let us not be so hasty here.

No other foundation can be laid but the rock of Christ! If the house of our life is founded upon the independent sand of self, it is destined for total ruin, even though it was built in the name of *Jesus*! Shocking but true, and it will not go away by refusing to look at it!

This independently owned and operated identity, which prides itself on traveling to the beat of a different drummer, is the very aspect of our soul that God considers worthless rubbish! However I submit to you, it is not only worthless to Him, it is altogether worthless to us as well! I am hopeful that we are becoming mature enough to realize that a will operating independent of the wisdom of God, is the sole *cause* for all of our personal suffering as well as that of the world!

That independent identity that we have clothed ourselves with up to this time is a lie of the first magnitude. The truth is we are, and always have been, fully dependent on the Creator and Sustainer of the universe. In fact, our every breath is an ongoing gift of God! Except, most people have spent a lifetime building *their life* around this core lie of independence.

To date, our soul's most creative, although dubious, accomplishment is the pseudo-life-form known as the ego. Our mind created the person we have come to believe ourselves to be. Daily we have added to the content of how we have defined ourselves. Each of us has been creating a mental construct which embodies a concept of ourselves that it labels "my life." This is an illusion that is held together by a thin thread of false belief. The lie of independence forces us to view life as an imagined possession, a conceptualized treasure that must be guarded and protected. However, life is never an object that can be possessed in this manner. *Life is what we are! The very essence of our being is life in expression!* So my question would be, who is this that is attempting to possess you?

Things that make you go, "Hmmmmm."

> Save others, snatching them out of the fire; and on some have mercy with fear, hating even the garment polluted by the flesh. (Jude 1:23)

The time has come to *voluntarily* shed this useless garment of independence and become consciously clothed in the mind of Christ. Independence is not fireproof!

> Behold, I am coming like a thief. Blessed is the one who stays awake and keeps his clothes, so that he will not walk about naked and men will not see his shame. (Revelation 16:15)

Please note that independent identity and individual identity are completely dissimilar. The word *individual* actually means "not dividable or whole." Our true identity in wholeness is only to be found in conscious union with our Creator. Our Father dwells within each of us, yet for all the clamor of an unruly mind, most are only marginally aware of it. What most people have yet to find out is that they were created to be a unique expression of the infinite personality of God who fills all things everywhere with Himself! Therefore, everything that we *think* we know about ourselves is a misperception and a misrepresentation of this greater reality. I believe it was our dear brother J. Preston Eby who said, "Man was created to be a container of God, and God intends on being our only content."

We will never experience any satisfaction in our earthly existence until we have found our identity sanctified in the infinite being of our Father!

> You will make me know the way of life. In Your presence is fullness of joys; at Your right hand are pleasures forever. (Psalms 16:11)

The fire of God is consuming every vestige of independence. Actually, it is the *notion* of independence that is being destroyed. This is *only an idea* that has lodged itself in the alienated consciousness of man. Our Father is engaged in a *cleanup operation* as in the refining process we have — the purging of the dross.

Nothing of value shall be lost, but we shall rather be, in every way, made whole and pure: a spotless, fully sanctified body of people. *Praise be to our Lord!*

> Behold, I am sending My messenger, and He will clear the way before Me. And the Lord whom you are seeking shall suddenly come to His temple, even the Angel of the Covenant, in whom you delight. Behold, He comes, says Jehovah of Hosts. But who can endure the day of His coming? And who will stand when He appears? For He is like a refiner's fire and like fuller's soap. And He shall sit as a refiner and purifier of silver; and He shall purify the sons of Levi and purge them like gold and like silver, that they may be presenters of a grain offering in righteousness to Jehovah. (Malachi 3:1-3)

Filled with His fullness, we shall then present the wheat of our souls fully winnowed of any chaff of rebellion. In absolute joy, we shall find our will perfectly unified with the will of the Lord. Amen.

The Proper Use of the Will

Human nature, being what it is, seems to make us vulnerable to being continually off balance. We all seem to have this tendency. Rather than merely compensating, we overcompensate whenever we perceive some imbalance. The net result is that we are still out of balance, looking at the world from the opposite pole. This is often true concerning this matter of the will.

For instance, my wife recently realized that all the effort she was expending trying to conform to an external code of conduct was a willful abstraction of the self. While this was true, it was through reactionary thinking that she overcompensated. Essentially she threw her hands up in an attitude of "If you want me to change, Lord, you are going to have to do it." My fair one was not realizing that this in itself is just as willful, albeit subtle.

Jesus said in Matthew 7:21, "Not every one that saith to me, Lord, Lord, shall enter into the kingdom of heaven; but he that doeth the will of my Father who is in heaven."

We can see from this that the responsibility for the doing of "Father's will" is clearly upon those who claim His lordship. Here again, a problem arises from our blindness.

By not recognizing the difference between doing *our own will* in Jesus' name (which is an ego-motivated religious relationship) and doing the will of the Father (which is a love-motivated spiritual relationship).

Nothing can ever be done by anyone at anytime outside of an exercise of will. We cannot even move our pinkie. The Holy Spirit is the *paraklētos* — the helper, not the doer. Man's problem is not that he has a will, but rather what is controlling it. Is the ego, the carnal mind-made self, in control? Alternatively, has the fully formed mind of Christ wrested control from this usurper? In regard to this question of control, there can be no mixture; it is one or the other!

Currently we are in a transition period. So living life in this role, as a *transformable lump of clay,* means that presently the only legitimate use of our will is *found by* humbly *setting ourselves in agreement* with the light Father has given.

We need to realize that primarily, this is an alignment of our heart. Our conscious mind may take notice of this alignment, but it does not initiate it. All of our outward actions in word or deed then become a completely effortless response to the internal alignment of our heart. We are merely moving and breathing in the Spirit of our Father's will that has been established in our heart.

I cannot offer better advice than to "know thyself." In this, *ruthless honesty* is our greatest ally!

> Draw near to God and He will draw near to you. Cleanse your hands, you sinners; and purify your hearts, you double-minded. (James 4:8)

> Then they said to Him, What may we do that we may work the works of God? Jesus answered and said to them, This is the work of God, that you believe into Him whom that One sent. (John 6:28-29; Literal Translation)

When we have done our "work" to set ourselves in total agreement, believing *into* whatever level of truth has been revealed to us, it places us into relationship with our Father's word that is no longer conflicted. Being in alignment to *truth* enables us to naturally walk it out in the "way" that we relate to the world at large. Therefore, this establishes our Father's will in our *life* as a present reality.

"Voila!" We have *growth*. Amazingly, no religious effort or conscious striving was required!

A growing branch is the only evidence there can be
of abiding in the supply of the vine.

For it is this restful abiding
that is the sum and substance of Father's will.

The Emotions of the Soul

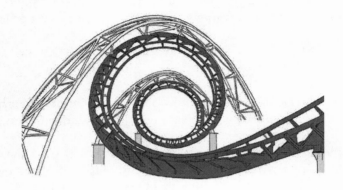

Oh the highs, oh the lows, oh the thrills and frightful chills — first this way, then that way, over and around, and upside down as we fly through the triple loop. Everyone loves a roller coaster. Well, almost everyone. It certainly isn't boring. One might even say it is exhilarating! It draws up from our well of emotions experiences of apprehension, anxiety, gleeful anticipation, or joyous rapture in some, sheer terror in others. In a word *fun*! There is a multibillion dollar industry out there that exists solely to cater to the needs of emotional junkies. You know, like me and you.

"Vanity, vanity," says the preacher.

Actually, a roller coaster serves to be a good analogy for the emotional life we experience in the world. It is this thrill ride that fuels the addictive nature of man. Every thriving ego will exhibit addictive behavior in some form or another, whether it is fast cars, food, alcohol, drugs, music, sports, work, gambling, religion, sex, violence, victimhood, ad infinitum. Whenever one digs deep enough, what is found driving these addictions is some emotionally backed demand dictating their life. The ego has manifold appetites!

People indulge themselves in this manner because of how it makes them feel for a short while. This covers the spectrum from the sublime to the dangerous. Our prisons are full of souls that committed crimes simply because they felt like it. Charting one's life by one's feelings inevitably proves a poor compass — in spite of what our culture might enjoin on you with "If it feels good, do it." *Webster* defines emotion in this way:

Emotion
emo'tion, noun [Latin. emotio; emoveo, to move from]

1. Literally, a moving of the mind or soul; hence, any agitation of mind or excitement of sensibility.

2. In a philosophical sense, an internal motion or agitation of the mind which passes away without desire; when desire follows, the motion or agitation is called a passion.

3. Passion is the sensible effect, the feeling to which the mind is subjected, when an object of importance suddenly and imperiously demands its attention.

Emotions are very potent thought forms that have the ability to elicit a bodily response or feeling. Our emotions trigger complex physiological changes in the chemistry of the body. Then in a feedback loop, we experience ourselves moved in one direction or another by the neurochemical messengers coursing through our veins. These messengers stimulate bodily feelings, and so we find ourselves feeling happy or sad, pensive or relaxed, etc.

The emotional nature of our soul is an absolutely wonderful part of our being. It really is the frosting on the cake. The ability to feel emotion has the capacity to make us vulnerable, or as strong as a lion, depending upon the individual and the circumstances in which we find ourselves.

As individuals, our emotional makeup is probably the most fascinating and unique aspect of our personhood, for it flavors how we perceive the world about us. This preprogrammed makeup has the power to strongly influence and shape our personality. Every person has a unique "emotional fingerprint" composed of various weaknesses, strengths, and sensitivities.

Our God truly is a God of variety, and if you doubt this for an instant, take a good long look into the ocean. When I see some of these strange and beautiful creatures, I am forced to exclaim in wonder, "What were you thinking, Lord?!"

Our Achilles' Heel

Have you ever noticed that you do not seem well-equipped to cope with some of the emotionally charged creatures found swimming the waters of your soul? Finding ourselves confronted with peculiar animals of a predatory nature such as anger, rage, or lust (covetousness). These great fish are always ready to swallow us up! Also found, although lurking in the shadows, are more insecure creatures such as fear, guilt, and dread.

We find this emotional menagerie so impossible to cope with because *we were never designed to handle them.* It is certain that our ego will never be able to tame them! These wild fight/flight abstractions of the beastly carnal mind were *imposed upon humanity,* specifically so we could come to experience the godless futility of our separated independent identity.

> For the creation was subjected to futility, not willingly, but because of Him who subjected it, in hope. (Romans 8:20)

Our experience of the futility of our upside-down carnality brings about what is called *pain.* Yet our pain is only a messenger, albeit a messenger that we are only too willing to have lose its head! Although, try as we might, this tactic does not work because, as with all of God's designs, futility is perfect. Another messenger will always be dispatched! That is, until we stop our willful denial of the message, pain will continue to be our constant companion!

So what vitally important message might pain carry for us? Well, when we finally get around to listening to the message of pain, we hear it telling us to look around and see where we are. Imploring us to notice the foul stench in the air and see how our feet are mired in our own clay as we laboriously feed the swine of our carnal nature. The incredible life-saving message that our pain carries is "Remember your father!" This loving reminder has always been meant to drive us home in the humility of servanthood!

Well then, the happy day has come for the prodigal to finally be separated from the swine of his carnal nature. In this, we must know that we cannot come fully into our Father's presence with a string of favored piglets walking in our footsteps! Is that *bacon I* hear crackling?

> Then Moses said, "I pray You, show me Your glory!" And He said, "I Myself will make all My goodness pass before you." But He said, "You cannot see My face, for no man can see Me and live!" (Exodus 33:18-19a & 20)

> Blessed are the pure in heart, for they shall see God. (Matthew 5:8)

In the garden, Adam was told that it was for *his sake* that the ground was cursed, and *in pain, he would partake of the fruit of it.* I believe there is ample cause to rethink whether our Heavenly Father was heaping shame upon His Son. Personally, I am fully persuaded that every word spoken in judgment was making a loving and necessary provision for the ultimate salvation of man, all the way down to his physical *flesh*!

It was with great purpose that God the Father subjected the world to futility. Ultimately, it shall not have been in vain. When in the restoration of all things, God, to the praise of His Glory, will have a people tried-and-true who are "infinitely" wiser.

The former things will not come to mind, but they will never be forgotten any more than the pattern son Jesus will forget the marks He bares. However, when considering the glory of His character worked into us by a correct response to our pain, it does take on new meaning. The day we clearly see God's wisdom concerning this, every tear shall vanish!

> For it was fitting for Him, for whom are all things, and through whom are all things, in bringing many sons to glory, to perfect the author of their salvation through sufferings. (Hebrews 2:10)

> Now I can find joy amid my sufferings for you, and I fill up in my own person whatever is lacking in Christ's afflictions on behalf of His Body, the Church. (Colossians 1:24; Weymouth New Testament)

Some people spend their entire lives being externally focused. These precious souls are valiantly dedicated to solving the world's problem of suffering. Although all they can do about the world's issues is make some attempt to address the *effects of pain*. Treating effects while leaving root causes intact only ensures job security. There will always be more effects to treat. "You seek me for the loaves and fishes."

Efforts such as these do bring immediate relief to the downtrodden, but the relief is temporary. This approach is lacking in ability to bring lasting change. So pragmatically, it is tantamount to attempting to cure cancer through the application of a Band-Aid, albeit one with a very happy face. This is why Jesus said, "For you always have the poor with you, and whenever you wish, you can do good to them, but you do not always have Me."

Only in Christ do we find *the cure for the cause of pain*! Jesus came to show us *the way to disconnect from the source of our pain* (our ego) and once again become vitally connected with the source of our true life, the flowing river of life — our Father!

"Oh my gosh, Jesus, You took all our pain? Thank you! Thank you! Thank you! Hmmmmmm." This highly intoxicating idea is very appealing to our pain-beleaguered fleshly mind! However, if you buy into it, you will be stuck with total failure in the name of religion! The actual solution that Jesus provided runs completely counter to what is considered "common sense" to the natural mind! We have to lose to win! We are going to have to embrace our pain and move through it in the healing fire of love! Actually, we are going to have to stop hating the pain. In fact, we are in need of a change of heart toward those things that would despitefully use us on any level.

The Sum of the World's Wisdom

The sum of the world's wisdom is all calculated upon pain avoidance. Everything, from purchasing the comfort of a new car to the reason children join a gang, is based upon pain avoidance. The latter example would be a case of one pain overriding the relative importance of another. The pain of isolation and a sense of not belonging become greater than the pain of initiation.

When it comes to the subject of pain, the world, in general, majors in the Band-Aid approach mentioned previously. As with all carnal solutions, there is a darker side to the Band-Aid philosophy of life. I am referring specifically to those psychopharmacological do-gooders that have a magic bullet for every faithful messenger of pain known to man—off with his head!

> And the light of a lamp will not shine in you any longer; and the voice of the bridegroom and bride will not be heard in you any longer; for your merchants were the great men of the earth, because all the nations were deceived by your sorcery. (Revelation 18:23)

G5331 sorcery.

pharmakeia

far-mak-i'-ah

From G5332; medication (pharmacy), that is, (by extension) magic (literal or figurative): sorcery, witchcraft.

Once again, the manipulation of people and circumstances is witchcraft. Manipulation always brings deception! *Pain actually has a legitimate purpose in God's economy.* The very thought of that runs counterintuitive to the agenda of the carnal mind. *How dare I question the nobility of our modern medicine! Where would we be without it?* Indeed no one knows! Where would we be without the deception that took a once vital and powerful church and turned it to rely instead upon a god of chemistry?

All the nations have been deceived by our culture's lucrative pain-avoidance strategies. Chemical tranquilizers keep a huge section of the populace anesthetized to any truth their pain would testify to them. Yet because all they have done is remove the awareness of pain, there will always be other and even more bizarre effects due to the cause of pain remaining intact!

Babylon also dispenses a fine line of religious tranquilizers: carnal doctrines designed to keep the weak and the malnourished sound asleep. Pain-avoidance strategies are likewise just as lucrative in this arena, and I don't have to point any further than the highly successful "left-behind" phenomena. The false and divisive doctrine that it purports caters specifically to the pain-avoidance psychology so prevalent in our culture! My point is not to give the church a black eye, but rather to point out a basic earmark of our carnality as being escapism or pain avoidance at all costs, even if we have to lie to ourselves to accomplish it!

Now that the utterly bewitching subject of the rapture has been broached, if this book has found its way into the hands of an individual who actively embraces this kind of belief system, you may as well *stop reading*! Doubtful, such foolish Galatians comprehend what is being said! An honest imbecile is far wiser than an educated liar!

You say, where's the love in that? Well, love does wear some funny clothes. The Pharisees were divided over Jesus precisely because some were being pricked in their conscience. A few were actually repenting due to His scathing denouncements. Jesus continually made an open show of their destructive stupidity. His very word was a fiery ministration of God's love!

> Alas for you, Scribes and Pharisees, hypocrites, for you scour sea and land in order to win one convert—and when he is gained, you make him twice as much a son of Gehenna as yourselves. (Matthew 23:15)

> He said to His disciples, "It is inevitable that stumbling blocks come, but woe to him through whom they come! It would be better for him if a millstone were hung around his neck and he were thrown into the sea, than that he would cause one of these little ones to stumble. Be on your guard! If your brother sins [is off target], rebuke him; and if he repents, forgive him." (Luke 17:1-3)

The dual purpose of this fast-paced book is not to educate nor sway anyone. But then neither is it "theotainment"! This book has been written to clearly and without ambiguity open the truths that actually are contained in God's Word, and thereby expose and confront the stinking carcass of our carnality that would keep us blind to them! If you can't take the heat now, allow me to remind you that no one will be able to avoid His kitchen forever!

Turn to my reproof, Behold, I will pour out my spirit on you; I will make my words known to you. (Proverbs 1:23)

Let us pause and take a deep-cleansing breath in the Spirit.

As commonly taught, the doctrine of the rapture
is a mere extension of the outright
lie of *hell*
born from the *myth* of an angry and vengeful God!

Healing the Painful Breach in Our Psychology

Personally, I do not believe there is another aspect of my humanity upon which I have so enjoyed our Savior's touch as my emotional makeup. This life's pains, abrasions, hurts, and scars have taken a toll upon all of us. Resentment for a world that has so taken advantage, used and abused, and generally failed to appreciate or acknowledge us to one degree or another has poisoned our souls.

The word *resentment* is compound in nature and comes from two Latin roots: *re* – "to do again" and *sentos* – "to feel." The word literally means to feel again. Therefore, as long as we harbor resentment, we feel our negativity again and again and again. Each time our bodies, as well as our souls, receive a fresh dose of poison. This is not very conducive to spiritual growth, and hence, we need to have the balm of Gilead applied by the Great Physician. Thank you, Lord.

Resentment is actually a covert form of contempt. Overt contempt of someone or something is a conscious act of which we are fully aware. This causes much pain as we work through the intense feelings we have attached to our personal issues. Many times after processing these feelings and resolving to make a conscious effort to forgive, there are some lingering secret resentments (stored emotional reaction patterns).

The act of someone carelessly stomping on my toe might be forgiven outwardly. Yet unbeknownst to me, I may harbor some deep feeling based in a value judgment about this individual that tends to influence my attitude toward people in general. Therefore, we must ask ourselves whether we have our emotions, or do they instead have us?

It is my earnest desire to become a more loving person. Yet I seemingly find that these dark emotions are willfully conspiring against that desire. Oh, "who shall deliver me from the body of this death?"

> But if I do that which I desire not to do, it can no longer be said that it is I who do it, but the sin which has its home within me does it. (Romans 7:20)

Sin: A Being or a Doing?

As humans, we are neither bad nor evil, but *we are cohabiting with a body of highly charged negative energy*. An emotionally fabricated being left unchallenged has a God-given mandate to kill us (Ezekiel 18:20)! We know that, ultimately, the wages of all that is not of faith brings death. Along the way, however, this darker side of our ego brings home a steady paycheck of mental, emotional, and physical disease.

Silently, we have somewhat accepted this as our lot in life! Feeling helpless and hopeless, religion notwithstanding, we have learned to cope by hiding from our growing body of pain.

Truthfully, there is great hope. I would like to share an empowering secret with you. Have you ever noticed that in our proceeding verse, Romans 7:20, Paul disassociated himself from sin? He clearly made a distinction between his true self and this body of sin (death) that resided within him.

Nowadays, Paul's apparent "devil-made-me-do-it" cavalier stand would undoubtedly get him thrown out of our modern self-help groups. Why, I can hear the choir now: "Paul, how dare you not take the responsibility for your own actions. You're in denial, son!" I submit to you, what Paul was actually doing was drawing a clear distinction between the portion of himself that *can be responsible* from the part that *will never be responsible*.

> No one who is born of God practices sin, because His seed abides in him; and he cannot sin, because he is born of God. (1 John 3:9)

By making this distinction, Paul severed all of the illusory strings of guilt that seemingly attached the *new man* with his ancient *body of sin*. I testify to you that if you also will do this, it will put you in a greatly empowered position. From the advantage of this elevated position, you can begin to dismantle the hateful body of sin (pain) that lodges within you!

Knowing this, that our old self *was crucified* with Him, *in order that* our *body of sin* might be done away with, so that we would no longer be slaves to sin. (Romans 6:6; italics mine)

But if I do that which I desire not to do, *it can no longer be said that it is I who do it,* but the sin which has its home within me does it. (Romans 7:20; italics mine)

Do you see it? The distinction that is made in Romans 6:6 between the *old self* which *was crucified* and the *body of sin which remains to be dealt with* – might be done away with. Then in Romans 7:20, we find Paul in the very process of realizing that in addition to this understanding, there is a distinction to be made between the *new man*, which has been created in righteousness and true holiness, and this yet troublesome body of sin. "It can no longer be said that it is I who do it, but the sin which has its home within me does it."

Yes, the old self was crucified, but he left behind all of his belongings! Besides the deep emotional imprint from the pain itself, there are well-established patterns of negative thinking associated with it. Accumulated pain drives all kinds of irrational attitudes, distorted beliefs, crazy unreasonable fears, out-of-balance appetites, and emotional trigger points (our buttons). These unwanted manifestations and a host of other unhealthy conditions all seem to have a life of their own!

Well, these destructive patterns definitely do have a life of their own! However, it is only because they have been thoroughly recorded into the fleshly memory of a living soul! Truly, we are but impressionable clay.

As sons of the Most High, one of our biggest hurdles is dealing with our tendency to continue to misidentify with the history of sin, pain and destructive patterns that have been *imprinted* upon our memory. Our tendency to identify with our pain is why making a clear distinction becomes crucial. Because until we have actually made this distinction, the best we can do is wrestle with our lifelong sparring partner called sin.

Striving in this manner always ends in a draw, though it constantly leaves our ego challenged to redouble its effort trying to procure the victory over its own darker side! It's an empty chasing after the wind that enables the ego to maintain its sense of legitimacy! Internally, this drama furnishes us with the impression that we are doing all we can to be godly. Yet it will never explain why a tangible victory is forever just out of reach!

After making a clear distinction between that which is born of God and that which has been born out of fear, we are empowered to dismantle this unwanted houseguest piece by piece: "that our body of sin might be done away with." Furthermore, it might be a very useful bit of insight to realize this is exactly how this Little Frankenstein was built up in our life—piece by piece.

How do you dismantle it? Glad you asked! Well, it just so happens that all the nuts and bolts that hold this robotlike creature together are all one size, and fortunately, we have the magic wrench that fits. That amazing wrench is called forgiveness. If I may head something off at the pass, the application of forgiveness that I am speaking of here has little to do with the world that exists outside of us! It rather has much to do with *the world that has been reproduced in us*!

Just under the surface of our conscious awareness lurks the body of pain that we have accumulated over the course of our lifetime. This painful child of sin is made up of every form of ire known by man: little snippets of hate, jealousy, fear, loneliness, doubt, insecurity, rage, isolation, rejection, anger, disappointment, abandonment ad infinitum. To further compound things, these intense feelings are tangled up with a long-forgotten mountain of suppressed guilt, shame, and grudge experiences.

All of this stays under the radar, so to speak; that is, until some hapless soul pushes one of our buttons and stimulates the ego's darker side. When this happens, the self-preserving ego will lash out at the world, protecting some area of pain that resonates with current events. Accumulated pain is the dark energy that drives our mutual failure in our interpersonal relations! Unconsciously, we associate people in our current experience with vague images in our mind of people who have hurt us in the past.

The vessel that harbors this negativity suffers more damage than the image receiving our rage! By venting upon an image in our memory, we unwittingly pour this foulness upon our own souls.

About now you may be asking, where is one supposed to start with this tangled ball of emotional knots? We will get back to the practical application of love's tools shortly. Stay with me, though, because I've not presented the full picture yet.

When it comes to the sticky subject of sin, most people have an image in their minds of some heavenly scribe that has been very busy keeping tabs on them ever since they stole their first cookie. By now, they are fairly sure that their personal volume resembles something more on the order of an unabridged *Webster's Dictionary*.

Relax, my friend. This imaginary book is not on display somewhere in heaven. It doesn't even exist. From God's perspective, "as far as the east is from the west, so far has He removed our transgressions from us" (Psalm 103:12).

Now, from our own perspective, we get to live with a consciousness of transgression with all of its associated *pain*. This is openly displayed. *We are the books that are known and read of all men.* In fact, the souls of men are the very record books that are opened onto judgment.

> Therefore do not go on passing judgment before the time, but wait until the Lord comes who will both bring to light the things hidden in the darkness and disclose the motives of men's hearts; and then each man's praise will come to him from God. (1 Corinthians 4:5)

Faithfully recorded within the pages of our own soul is every motivation and, to stay with the darker side of this, every transgression from the great cookie capers on. Largely, what the world gets to read is the influence that this growing body of unprocessed pain has upon every interpersonal transaction that we carry out.

The plastic facade that we try to put on to the world does more to fool ourselves than it does anyone else! Though, in the back of our minds, we already know this because this is a two-way street. We are constantly reading everyone else's book right through their well-practiced facade, and to put it mildly, we are not entirely pleased with all we read in them.

Well, do your best not to hold it against them. They helplessly accumulated their load of garbage in the same way that we did ours. Some might say, "The stuff written in So-and-so's book is way fouler than my own!" Really?

More than likely, the truth is we are much too distracted by the world to have ever given our own book much of an honest read!

When we realize the only remedy for the cause of pain is to forgive the world outright, we will be well on our way to a life of real peace. It is only within the extended framework of forgiveness that we may begin to clear the hidden pain in the pages of our own book.

By dismantling our own monster through the transforming power of forgiveness, we again become as little children. Then we will be able to say just as our Lord,

> The ruler of the world is coming, and he has nothing in Me. (John 14:30)

The audience of the world waits eagerly to read the Lamb's life expressed in us.

> *For all can see that you are a letter of Christ* entrusted to our care and written not with ink, but with the Spirit of the ever-living God — and not on tablets of stone, but on human hearts as tablets. (2 Corinthians 3:3; italics mine)

This is not a contrived behavior according to some code of ethics that "all can see." Rather, it is a profound change in the core of our being that effortlessly manifests God's grace, love, and forgiveness before the wondering eyes of the world!

Human heart = deepest part of the mind—the wellspring of all the issues of life!

When you hear His voice, "do not harden your hearts" according to the indoctrination you have suffered. Keep the clay of your heart impressionable, moist with the water of life. This receptive attitude of heart is the only one that you can ever trust!

SIN Comes in Three Flavors

Previously I defined SIN as being self-inflicted nonsense. Well, it is nonsense; and it comes in three flavors: expression, suppression, and repression. By these, we are *shaped, molded, and conformed to the customs of the world.* Expressive sin really needs very little explanation. Expressive sins are those mutual actions that get us into so much trouble in our interpersonal affairs. They cause us relational pain and add to our suppressed guilt load. The latter two are responsible for driving much of our unconscious action.

Do you recall that I said that we do not comprehend the mechanics of how we are conformed to the world, or what we are currently doing that perpetuates our conformity? Sins of suppression are the well-practiced coping mechanisms we have developed to deal with the destructive energies of such strong emotions such as jealousy, hate, anger, and rage. If we were to allow this energy expression, it might result in maiming someone, the destruction of property, or homicide. We also intentionally suppress things like guilt, desire, loneliness, fear, and honesty.

It is by a conscious decision that we suppress these things, although it is not by choice because choice implies another option. Our default-coping behaviors are so proven by practice that the idea of another way seems strange and alien. All other options are to be regarded with much suspicion. For this is how we have learned to get by: first by suppressing the energy that we are not equipped to deal with and then covering it over with all the activities of daily living. We attempt to lose ourselves in TV, work, hobbies, sports, family, church functions, or any combination to make the pain go away. This works! So we think, although it doesn't really work. The only thing that happens is we lose touch with the pain that is trying to tell us something. It is like stuffing a bunch of rags in that annoying fire-alarm bell. Ah, relief, yes! But what of the fire?

When we lose touch in this manner with the pain of unprocessed out-of-balance energies, our SIN is repressed, and the result is unconsciousness. It is from this nonsense that our private Little Frankenstein is made.

Ever found yourself saying, "I don't know what possessed me to say or do that"? Do you ever experience your mind driving you a little crazy with endless chatter and nonsense thoughts? How is it that a song is so easily stuck in our head? The mind is merely attempting to keep a cover on its unprocessed energy! This manufactured static is jamming the airwaves, preventing the repressed pain from surfacing! The ego-driven mind is only doing what it subconsciously deems necessary to keep the pressure corked in the bottle! The problem is we cannot keep a lifetime of defiling energy stored in our vessel without it destroying the temple. "There is a way that seems right to a man, but its end is the way of death." *It is by this type of soulish wisdom that we are conformed to the customs of the world*!

> Do you not know that you are a temple of God and that the Spirit of God dwells in you? If any man destroys the temple of God, God will destroy him, for the temple of God is holy, and that is what you are. Let no man deceive himself. *If any man among you thinks that he is wise in this age, he must become foolish, so that he may become wise.* For the wisdom of this world is foolishness before God. For it is written, "He is *the one who catches the wise in their craftiness.*" (1 Corinthians 3:16-19; italics mine)

Nonetheless, *God* is not out to get any one!
Once again, this is purely self-inflicted nonsense.

Hypothesis:

1. Our *spirit* in a holy union with an all-consuming *God*
2. Our *soul* (mind, will, and emotions)
3. The *ego* or *man of sin* (stored body of negative energy lodged in our soul)

They are all sharing the same vessel (body temple).

Questions:

What do you suppose will happen if we refuse to take up our cross and are willing to tolerate our soul being entangled with the "man of sin?" Do you really believe it wise to experiment?

108

Option 1:

Through faithful trust, our heart aligns in our Father's intention, plan, and purpose. Thus, we become willing to have this chameleon exposed.

Result:

We embark on an amazing journey of self-discovery. Along the way, our Father orchestrates life's circumstances to bring every repressed pain to the surface. The aspect of us that has identified with the pain is *exposed* and *consumed* in the fire of His love.

> Then that lawless one will be *revealed* whom the Lord will slay with the breath of His mouth and *bring to an end by the appearance of His coming*. (2 Thessalonians 2:8; italics mine)

Free and at peace, we stand with the Lamb as a victorious overcomer, the name of His Father written on our forehead! (His Divine Nature written throughout our mind, will, emotions!) We take part in the first resurrection and with the richness of this fantastic journey also written into our soul for eternity, we reign with Christ throughout the millennium.

Option 2:

Falsely believing that it is just too much to deal with, we cowardly continue to entertain escapist beliefs and/or personal codes and so further suppress anything that might remotely resemble pain! No elephant standing here!

Result:

The status quo remains! As a "believer," we continue to stumble in defeat to the man of sin. Ultimately, he receives his wages and takes us out with him. We enter the afterlife with our load of undealt-with pain and its associated aggression still recorded into our soul. The next thing we see is a great white throne where books are being opened, including our own book. Here, we also see that another book is being opened, which is the life of the Lamb. Only to our great amazement, we discover that it has all been written into the *souls of His overcoming remnant.* As we peer into our own book, we will compare the things recorded with the life of the Lamb recorded in His book. In that moment, "we *shall know even as we are known*"! As all of our illusions are "cut in pieces" only one word shall cross our lips — *oh!* However, in that simple acknowledgment, cleansing will have already begun!

> And the Lord said, "Who then is the faithful and sensible steward, whom his master will put in charge of his servants, to give them their rations at the proper time? Blessed is that slave whom his master finds so doing when he comes. Truly I say to you that he will put him in charge of all his possessions. But if that slave says in his heart, 'My master will be a long time in coming,' and begins to beat the slaves, both men and women, and to eat and drink and get drunk; the master of that slave will come on a day when he does not expect him and at an hour he does not know, and *will cut him in pieces, and assign him a place with the unbelievers.* And *that slave who knew his master's will and did not get ready or act in accord with his will, will receive many lashes,* but the one who did not know it, and committed deeds worthy of a flogging, will receive but few. *From everyone who has been given much, much will be required; and to whom they entrusted much, of him they will ask all the more. I have come to cast fire upon the earth; and how I wish it were already kindled!*" (Luke 12:42-49; italics mine)

But for the *cowardly* and *unbelieving,* and those having become foul, and murderers, and fornicators, and sorcerers, and idolaters, and all the *lying ones*, their part will be in the Lake burning with fire and brimstone, which is the second death. (Revelation 21:8; Literal Translation; italics mine)

Undoubtedly, you have noticed that I am not giving any quarter to the flesh. We need to remember that here we are no longer speaking about a wonderful period of grace, whereby we may work out the salvation of our soul. Here we are speaking about an ultimate judgment unto a mandatory cleansing—a complete and total resolution of the issue.

Lose your ego-driven life now, or *lose it later.* First or second death is entirely your call! However, there is no salvation available for the untransformed *carnal* mind, will, and emotions! Only the new creation shall inherit the *kingdom!* The only one that has ever been *lost* is the *son of perdition,* the traitor of the Adamic mind-set—the ego!

All believers have received Christ as crucified for them. Therefore, all can rejoice in the mutual joy of this wonderful life-saving gift. Those to whom our Lord grants the title overcomer mirror this gift and have come to know through experience that their opinions, attitudes, ideas, and beliefs are all crucified in Christ. For them, this is not some tacit intellectual idea. They willingly experience denying the ego, and bit by bit, they consciously lay down this life in the fire. This death, or this cleansing of the temple, is established throughout their earthly sojourn in grace! Eventually, the Lord of glory fills the vacancy where previously only an independent identity impudently stood.

I have been crucified with Christ; *and it is no longer I who live, but Christ lives in me*; and the life which I now live in the flesh I live by faith in the Son of God, who loved me and gave Himself up for me. (Galatians 2:20; italics mine)

Let the one who does wrong, still do wrong; and the one who is filthy, still be filthy; and let the one who is righteous, still practice righteousness; and the one who is holy, still keep himself holy. *Behold, I am coming quickly, and My reward is with Me, to render to every man according to what he has done.* (Revelation 22:11-12; italics mine)

This is a long drawn-out way to say, "Go ahead!" Our Father—through the written word, through His Son Jesus, and through the dispensing of His Holy Spirit—has given us all the input we require. In response to what He has given, He will allow us to be or do whatever seems right in our own eyes. We are free to abide in His Word or reject it!

About now, our carnally understood doctrines might pipe up and say, "I thought my salvation was about grace and not about works!" That would be totally correct! Actually, this has never been in question.

Those who make this assertion have enough light to realize that we cannot earn our salvation through the "works of the law." Any motivation to make ourselves more acceptable only makes us self-righteous. Truly, this is not acceptable! It is most ironic that many will spend their lives on this dead-end road while maintaining a doctrine against it!

Our salvation is the totally free gift of the overwhelming love of God! It is by grace we have been saved (past tense, done deal!). *We cannot do anything to earn it!* In fact, we never had anything to do with it! Jesus did it all for all! Therefore, a growing number are finally coming to an understanding that *neither can we do anything to lose it*! For we cannot incur a debt that is greater than this gift!

It is most important to remember that the essence of who we are is spirit and not the virtual thought stuff of soul! Because by knowing that our spirits are eternally secure, it precludes the possibility of wrong motivation in the working out of the salvation of our soul!

The transforming of our *soul* unto salvation is unequivocally about work! The only things in question are (1) Is the motivation of my heart based in fear or love? (2) Whose work or works are being done? (3) Where do my responsibilities end and the Lord's begin?

> For we are His workmanship, created in Christ Jesus for good works, which God prepared beforehand so that we would walk in them. (Ephesians 2:10)

It takes a peculiar mind-set to step into this! Only to the degree that we are willing to *allow Christ access* are we ever established as *His workmanship*! Those who will someday hear the Lord declare to them, *"I never knew you; depart from me, you who practice lawlessness"* never allowed the Lord any freedom in their lives.

Therefore, "He *must* increase, but I *must* decrease!" "Nevertheless I live, yet not I, but Christ lives in me." You see, any "good works" that we eventually walk in are only wrought by the increase of the mind of Christ expressed through the temple of our body.

All of these "good works" are external to us, and none of them is our work per se. This work is only accomplished through a genuine humility of mind that is fully cognizant of being indwelt by another.

> Do you not believe that I am in the Father, and the Father is in Me? The words that I say to you I do not speak on My own initiative, but *the Father* abiding in Me *does His works*. (John 14:10; italics mine)

Without a doubt, the world receives a blessing from God's children when they are walking in the enjoyment of our Father's work in their lives! The wonderful work of a sanctified heart and mind in the attitude of a servant cannot help but be a blessing to those with whom they come in contact! Still this is Father's work!

> For it is God who is at work in you, both to will and to work for His good pleasure. (Philippians 2:13)

But there is another category of work for which we must claim personal responsibility.

> For no man can lay a foundation other than the one which is laid, which is Jesus Christ. Now if any man builds on the foundation with gold, silver, precious stones, wood, hay, straw, each man's work will become evident; for the day will show it because it is to be revealed with fire, and the fire itself will test the quality of each man's work. If any man's work which he has built on it remains, he will receive a reward. If any man's work is burned up, he will suffer loss; but he himself will be saved, yet so as through fire. (1 Corinthians 3:11-15)

There are only two kinds of works represented here: flammable and fireproof. All flammable works are *ego motivated* and share in that fictional being's destiny. Those of a fireproof nature are representative of the progressive work of the cross. (Gold, *one hundredfold*; silver, *sixtyfold*; precious stones, *thirtyfold*.) This work is the internal sacrifice of our ego-self to our cross. This incremental work of death will have an indirect impact on the world, but it has a far more direct and immediate bearing on the authority of the kingdom manifesting within and around us!

Through the ongoing death of our ego, our soul then becomes ever more established upon the life of the rock! Therefore, our cross is an incremental work of not only *death* but *life* upon our soul.

We must remember that our sacrificial life, established on the foundation of Christ, makes us an honored vessel in the Master's hand, no matter where we are in this progressive process.

The Currency of Transformation

Willingness is the kingdom's currency of transformation!

> I advise you to buy from Me gold refined by fire. (Revelation 3:18)

Gold is a symbolic reference to divinity or divine nature. *Fire,* in this instance, is a reference to adversity from the wickedness that is rampant in the world.

The golden loving nature of our Father's divinity may only be purchased by a willing sacrifice of everything that comes so natural to our contrary ego-driven nature! Whenever evil manifests at our doorstep, and we refrain from blind reaction, making a conscious choice to respond in love, our Father's golden character is inscribed upon our heart.

This takes the willing sacrifice of any and all ideas of personal rights, self-pity, anger, resentment, and cursing. It is the complete sacrifice of everything that the ego uses to justify its self-centered existence.

We do not possess, nor will we ever possess the power to transform ourselves! However, it is well within the power of a hard heart to delay it! In this, we must be very careful, or we may soon find that we have delayed it onto the grave!

God's glorious kingdom can only manifest in the earth through transformed souls. Willingness is the singular prerequisite key to this transformation! Yet, our Lord is not the least bit interested in some concept that our carnal mind might entertain about willingness. He waits and watches the heart and will take immediate action the moment He sees the willingness to embrace the cross. We may easily fool ourselves in this, but praise God, we will never fool Him!

Overcoming the opinion of the world, the opinion of our flesh, and the opinion of the devil is a lot of work and, frequently, not a whole lot of fun. Rewarding beyond ability to describe, yes, but not fun! This is why we have been told to count the cost! As much as is possible, know what you are getting into before you even begin! Next, realize that this is an *all-or-nothing lifetime commitment to whatever it takes*! When you are ready, commit everything that you are and everything that you have to the accomplishing of it! Do this, and you will never hear anyone say, "This one began to build and was not able to finish."

> Another also said, "I will follow You, Lord; but first permit me to say good-bye to those at home." But Jesus said to him, "No one, after putting his hand to the plow and looking back, is fit for the Kingdom of God." (Luke 9:61-62)

Regardless of how difficult or daunting the process may seem, the fact remains that the overcomer's death is a graceful transition because it is accomplished incrementally. We are afforded the opportunity to gradually process the surfacing pain through the fiery transmuting power of love! In my limited understanding, I cannot imagine what the Lake of Fire will be like for those foolish virgins who chose to go that way! This I do know, the unbelieving shall be as naked spirits. They are saved, yes, but they shall suffer the complete loss of everything in their untransformed soul! It is not the loss of the dimension of the soul itself, much more like reverting to the blank slate of a newborn baby. An entire lifetime lived, but absolutely nothing to show for it. All of their identity, personality, and memory they cunningly and painstakingly clothed themselves with will be completely dis-integrated! Actually, this is an extraordinary display of our Father's love as it is the best that can be done for them. However, think soberly about this a minute: If you wipe the hard drive of a computer clean, it has all the practical value of an expensive paperweight!

> Though the wicked is shown favor, He does not learn righteousness; He deals unjustly in the land of uprightness and does not perceive the majesty of the Lord. (Isaiah 26:10)
>
> But by His word the present heavens [our souls] and earth [our bodies] are being reserved for fire, kept for the day of judgment and destruction of ungodly men. (2 Peter 3:7)

At the very core of the contention between those who teach the ultimate reconciliation of all and those who preach the doctrine of hell is a moronic failure to understand the difference between the spirit and the soul!

116

That and a small matter of an unprocessed body of pain demanding payback!

You are probably wondering where the believer might fit in between the polar opposites of *unbeliever* and *overcomer*. Answering that question is not as straightforward as you might think. I would have to ask, "What do you mean believer?" I have met many unbelieving people that name the name of Christ, and I have met many people that have been given the grace to see through the sham of religion and have rejected all labels, yet walk in His spirit!

Where one actually fits into the *final cleansing of all mankind*, no one is qualified to say, except for the individual himself. However, Jesus did give us a further indication about this when he divided all of humanity in the sum of these obscure sayings:

> For he who is not against us is for us. (Mark 9:40)

> He who is not with Me is against Me; and he who does not gather with Me, scatters. (Luke 11:23)

Unlike religion, there are simple defining limits set here. Implied within the bounds of these broad limits, there is a fertile field that stretches over the horizon. Regarding the King's harvest, Jesus said, "And others fell on the good soil and yielded a crop, some a hundredfold, some sixty, and some thirty."

Where does the believer fit in? Well, what are his intentions? It may help to realize that none will overcome accidentally!

> From the days of John the Baptist until now the kingdom of heaven suffers violence, and violent men take it by force. For all the prophets and the Law prophesied until John. (Matthew 11:12-13)

Just remember that to whatever degree our carnal nature remains intact is the degree to which we will suffer loss! Nevertheless, as motivating factors go, I think it wiser to keep one's eyes firmly fixed upon the prize of the high calling in Christ. As I personally do not count myself as having already attained, I cannot think of an unhappier fate than to be among those who, after preaching to others, are themselves rejected. I have heard it said, "It's better to aim high and miss than it is to aim low and hit." However, that philosophy is totally unacceptable! We have been instructed to uncompromisingly run *so as to attain* (1 Corinthians 9:24-27).

For those who've shown the grit to be reading yet, I heartily commend you. Although written only for your edification, I am well aware the nature of this word is hard to digest. These are the things of which Jesus spoke in John 16:12, saying, "I have many more things to say to you, but you cannot bear them now. But when He, the Spirit of truth, comes, He will guide you into all the truth; for He will not speak on His own initiative, but whatever He hears, He will speak; and He will disclose to you what is to come." Therefore, for those with ears to hear what the Spirit is saying, I rejoice on your behalf!

If this word meets with rejection, it makes little difference as I am no longer moved very much by the opinion of man! I am quite crucified to the world, and the world is crucified to me! I've only urged you to follow Christ in love! Yet the content of this oracle has a great deal of personal significance for those with a mind to accept or reject! Choose well.

I know that God's fire is actually in this word. Without question, it is destroying anything that threatens to bind our understanding! This is equally true for those who do not know what to make of it! Because His Word has the power and authority to burst our old wineskin, some will be looking for a new paradigm soon. The new one will be flexible enough to hold an expanding understanding!

Finally, for those who have been warmed by His fire, who have had the coals in their heart stirred, I declare that you are by no means "lukewarm." God will now begin a deeper work that produces the maturity of wholeness! *Expect change!*

Whom the Lord Loves, He Disciplines

Foolishness is bound up in the heart of a child; the rod of discipline will remove it far from him. (Proverbs 22:15)

This verse aptly describes how life is experienced as an overcoming son in training! The utterly foolish wisdom of the world (our carnality) is subconsciously bound up in the deepest part of the mind — the wellspring of all the issues of life. Without the chastening rod of correction, training us up in the way we should go, we cannot access what all is bound up in there! When our Loving Father puts us through the fires of life, He will sometimes bring extremely harsh circumstances to bear against us! However, this is no random act of violence. This crucible of circumstances is custom-tailored to resonate with some aspect of the body of pain tenaciously lodged in our heart! He told us that He would remove the heart of stone from our flesh and would give us a heart of flesh. But He never said that He would wave a magic wand over us to accomplish it. We not only face the challenge of dealing with our current circumstances in wisdom from love's toolbox, but we also will have to forgive a load of repressed emotional garbage. These long-forgotten emotional patterns have come bubbling to the surface from the depths of our carnality! Yet, we will not always be aware that we are dealing with this additional load.

But the Lord said to him, "Go, for *he is a chosen instrument of Mine*, to bear My name before the Gentiles and kings and the sons of Israel; for *I will show him how much he must suffer for My name's sake*." (Acts 9:15-16; italics mine)

Our Loving Father will never allow more than we can bear, but He will take us right to the edge for maximum growth potential! In addition to cleansing us from all of the unrighteousness we have stored up in our soul, He also is accomplishing an amazing transformation of our character. He will repeatedly squeeze us in what appears to be dire straits until we take our eyes off of this world and *permanently fix them upon Him*, forsaking all else! To never again take them off of him! Not even blinking! This is not a conscious exercise of the will. This is an attitude of heart that, though I am somewhat at a loss to describe, is effortless and becomes as automatic and natural as breathing!

Simply fixing our gaze upon Jesus, our Prince Leader in the faith, who will also award us the prize. He, for the sake of the joy which lay before Him, patiently endured the cross, looking with contempt upon its shame, and afterwards seated Himself — where He still sits — at the right hand of the throne of God. Therefore, if you would escape becoming weary and faint-hearted, compare your own sufferings with those of Him who endured such hostility directed against Him by sinners. In your struggle against sin you have not yet resisted so as to endanger your lives; and you have quite forgotten the encouraging words which are addressed to you as sons, and which say, "My son, do not think lightly of the Lord's discipline, and do not faint when He corrects you; for those whom the Lord loves He disciplines: and He scourges every son whom He acknowledges." The sufferings that you are enduring are for your discipline. God is dealing with you as sons; for what son is there whom his father does not discipline? And if you are left without discipline, of which every true son has had a share, that shows that you are bastards, and not true sons. (Hebrews 12:2-8)

He will bring a cacophony of chaos into our life: noise and confusion of every type and description until we learn to stop listening to the world and turn to the calm within. Repeated practice will have so sharpened and attuned our ears to His voice that His softest whisper appears as a loud clear call reverberating through our spirit.

He will bring huge obstacles into our path. Thus, offering immovable rocks to break our will. Rising to the challenge, our ego stubbornly redoubles its effort until broken and spent we permanently retire our will. Preferring instead His everlasting arms, we take our hands off our life. Come what may, we learn that our Father is in full control. With our implicit trust, we joyfully acknowledge His authority and come to honor His will above our own.

Our experiences in the fires of life will bring about in us a quality of character that could not be achieved in any other way! We shall come to know the feeling of being approved in His sight. We will know He is aware we have come to value those very trials: testing, purging, stripping, pruning, and burnings that are responsible for these profound changes in our character. We are grateful for His unrelenting attention to our life! In addition to this change in character, we discover new faculties and abilities that previously were unknown. A heightened sense of discernment and an awareness of His moving (quickening) in the affairs of men bring an enhanced sense of connectedness, even on a global scale. The ability to hear His singular voice speaking out of the din of humanity brings a new dimension to our relationship. The ability to trace His hand in all the affairs of men makes the world our oyster. Laid open to our view, it displays the most exquisite pearl, our precious brothers in tribulation.

Beloved, think it not strange concerning *the fiery trial which is to try you, as though some strange thing happened to you.* (1 Peter 4:12; italics mine)

Wherefore, let them that suffer according to the will of God, commit the keeping of their souls to him in well-doing, as to a faithful Creator. (1 Peter 4:19)

For our light affliction, which is but for a moment, worketh out for us a far more exceeding and eternal weight of glory. (2 Corinthians 4:17)

But the God of all grace, who hath called us to His eternal glory by Christ Jesus, *after ye have suffered a while, make you perfect, establish, strengthen, settle you.* (1 Peter 5:10; italics mine)

Bastards, Not True Sons: Part 1

> But as many as received Him, to them He gave the right to become
> children of God, even to those who believe in His name, who were
> born, not of blood nor of the will of the flesh nor of the will of man, but
> of God. [The translation children is politically correct nonsense, and it
> will distort your understanding, it should read sons!] (John 1:12-13)

He has given this right even to those who believe in His name! But
according to this, we are not considered a *son of God* simply because we
believe. Believing only gains us the right to follow on to know the Lord
and begin to mature.

"East is East, and West is West, and never the twain shall meet!" Do you
recall how I was alluding to the fact that our Western culture is isolated
from the understanding of what has been written out of an Eastern
mind-set? Well, to use a simply ridiculous euphemism, "we don't stand
a snowballs chance in hell" to understand John 1:12-13 from our Western
understanding! A clear understanding of this scripture is of *paramount
importance*!

> For I could wish that I myself were accursed, separated from Christ for the sake of my brethren, my kinsmen according to the flesh. (Romans 9:3)

> Who are Israelites, to whom belongs the adoption as sons, and the glory and the covenants and the giving of the Law and the temple service and the promises. (Romans 9:4)

> Whose are the fathers, and from whom is the Christ according to the flesh, who is over all, God blessed forever. Amen. (Romans 9:5)

Take a close look at Romans 9:4. Paul is speaking about the linage of Israel, *the natural heirs* to all of the promises. Why is it that he speaks of *their adoption*? How does this square with our Western understanding about adoption? Now then, if we do not understand "their adoption," how is it we expect to understand our own as a Gentile?

There are many verses in the New Testament that speak of adoption, but they are not speaking about the same concept that comes into your mind when you, as a Westerner, hear the word *adoption*! Jesus Himself is an adopted son!

> Now I say, as long as the heir is a child, he does not differ at all from a slave although he is owner of everything, but he is under guardians and managers until the date set by the father. (Galatians 4:1)

In the culture of this era's Jewish customs, the household was basically split down the middle. There was the *woman's side* of the home, with the responsibility of managing the domestic servants. It was a place for cooking and taking care of the children. Then there was the *head of the household's side* of the home, which was a place of peace and dignity. It was a quasisacred space set aside for learning Torah and for the conducting of family business. No immature children allowed!

In looking into how this is practiced today, when a male child reaches the age of thirteen years and one day, they call for a feast. A ceremony is held for the youngster called a bar mitzvah. In the Jewish culture of the time of Paul, a male child would then receive the status of an adult and a space would be made for him to live on the Father's side of the household. Here he would be completely weaned from his mother and younger siblings. He would set to work, learning Torah and being about his father's business. This is analogous to the day that you accepted Christ and made a commitment to be about your Father's business. Heavenly speaking, according to this, either Jesus was just a little precocious or, over the centuries, the age requirement changed.

During this time of learning and training, the youth, though he was an heir, was not yet considered a son. Always close by his father's side, it was an extended period of learning the family business. Thus, our pattern for life: "Jesus kept increasing in wisdom and stature, and in favor with God and men." For eighteen more years, Jesus would grow in stature and in the understanding of Himself in a true knowledge of Torah!

The Father's watchful eye is ever upon His son in training. When all of the attributes that were needed to faithfully administer the responsibilities of the family business were witnessed in a heart of uncompromising dedication, the Father then called for a great feast and invited all of the family and neighbors. During the celebration, the Son would be brought forward and presented to all in attendance with the acknowledgment of these words: "This is My beloved Son in whom I am well pleased." By this acknowledgment, he was *placed as a Son*! Along with this placement, he was given the Father's signet ring. By the implicit trust of the Father, he was invested with the privilege, right, and full authority to conduct business in the Father's name! Thus, he was said to be, what has been translated for us, *"adopted"*.

Concordance reference—G5206 Adoption
uihothesia

hwee-oth-es-ee'-ah

From a presumed compound of G5207 and a derivative of G5087; the placing as a son, that is, adoption (figuratively Christian sonship in respect to God): adoption (of children, of sons).

Bastards, Not True Sons: Part 2

Occasionally, a man would have a rebellious, undisciplined child who was never willing to submit to the training and develop the attributes that are needed to function in the authority of the father. This one would watch his younger brother come of age and then go on to enter the business with all the rights and privileges that according to birth order would have been his. "The elder shall serve the younger." The elder brother would never know the honor of hearing from the lips of his father the wonderful declaration to everyone, "This is My beloved Son in whom I am well pleased." He still is considered kin, but when it comes to the rights and privileges afforded to one that carries family authority, he might as well have bore someone else's name. "A bastard and not a true son!"

> But as many as received Him, to them *He gave the right to become children* of God, even to those who believe in His name, *who were born*, not of blood nor of the will of the flesh nor of the will of man, but of God. [The use of the word *children* in this verse is utter foolishness—"a child is born, but a son is given!"] (John 1:12-13)

As a believing child of God, you have *every right to become* a *son*, but you are "wretched, miserable, poor, blind, and naked" if you think manifest sonship is an automatic part of the package we received as a gift!

Personally, I can think of no greater irony than how appealing the concept of grace is to the flesh! The incredibly ironic thing about grace is that it is never extended to the flesh!

Perhaps, at the root of this illusion is an unconscious thought that somehow the Adamic race got away with something through the atoning work of the cross. This is patently untrue. Every man's spirit was crucified in Christ! Therefore, we all paid the debt we owed by virtue of Christ's atonement! The fact that Jesus went to the cross *as us* is overlooked when it is overshadowed by the elation that He went to the cross *for us!*

When our spiritual account was reconciled by this payment, it gave God an entrance to bring a work of grace into our life. The *good news* of grace is the power of God unto the salvation of our soul!

For I am not ashamed of the gospel, for it is the power of God for salvation to everyone who believes, to the Jew first and also to the Greek. (Romans 1:16)

It is through God's grace that we have been empowered to crucify the fleshly nature! Not behavior, mind you, but nature.

I desire to remind you—although the whole matter is already familiar to you—that the Lord saved a people out of the land of Egypt, but afterwards destroyed those who had no faith. (Jude 1:5; Weymouth New Testament)

It was through a lack of trust in their Father's loving care that these "saved" people refused to conquer the land. However, this object lesson was only a mere type and shadow of those who refuse to conquer (crucify) the flesh.

Any worldview that does not take this understanding into account is extremely nearsighted! Nonetheless, the destructive actions of God cannot be understood for what they are without a clear understanding of the difference between *soul* and *spirit*.

And Jesus said to them, "Therefore *every scribe who has become a disciple of the kingdom* of heaven is like a head of a household, *who brings out of his treasure things new and old.*" (Matthew 13:52; italics mine)

The world that we live in today affords us with many analogies that were not available in the apostle Paul's day. Our mutual experiences with today's computer culture may offer some help in visualizing the difference between the body, soul, and spirit.

Hardware, software, and user are all aspects to a functioning computer system. Some amazing things can be accomplished with a healthy well-configured system. However, if the operating system becomes corrupted, or if you load conflicting software, some very strange and aggravating behavior is likely to manifest.

Our body—with its nervous system and electrochemical biocomputer, the brain—is analogous to the physical hardware of a personal computer (PC).

Our soul — with all the virtual thought stuff of the mind: worldview, personal beliefs, attitudes, ideas, fears, faiths, and long-term memory of successes and failures — is analogous to the operating system and software programs running on a PC.

Our spirit is analogous to the operator or user of the PC.

Usually when problems develop with a computer system, they can be sorted out and corrected by enlisting the aid of a helper known as tech support. The time spent sorting out the offending conflicts or corruption is analogous to our current Age of Grace.

Sometimes, it is possible to get things so fouled up, either through the abuse of ignorance or through a "tare" known as a virus that the only effective thing that can be done is to reformat the hard drive!

In the reformatting process, all of the bits of information that made up the operating system and software programs are destroyed!

Often a user will perceive this as a loss, sometimes even a great loss, but it never destroys the user himself!

> For the LORD will rise up as at Mount Perazim, He will be stirred up as in the valley of Gibeon to do His task, His unusual task, and to work His work, His extraordinary work. And now do not carry on as scoffers, or your fetters will be made stronger; for I have heard from the Lord GOD of hosts of decisive destruction on all the earth. Give ear and hear my voice, Listen and hear my words. (Isaiah 28:21-23)

> For the time has come for judgment to begin, and to begin at the house of God; and if it begins with us, what will be the end of those who reject God's Good News? And *if it is difficult even for a righteous man to be saved*, what will become of irreligious men and sinners? Therefore also, *let those who are suffering in accordance with the will of God* entrust their souls in well-doing to a faithful Creator. (1 Peter 4:17-19; Weymouth New Testament; italics mine)

He who does not bellow the truth when he knows the truth makes himself the accomplice of liars and forgers. (Charles Péguy 1943)

A Man's Enemies

Do not think that I came to bring peace on the earth; *I did not come to bring peace, but a sword.* For I came to set a man against his father, and a daughter against her mother, and a daughter-in-law against her mother-in-law; and *a man's enemies will be the members of his household.* (Matthew 10:34-36; italics mine)

Without a doubt, due to the hardness of man's carnal heart, we have seen religion become a cause for contention and, sometimes, even bitter warfare within the family structure of mankind. In this verse, as with all of Jesus' sayings, there is a deeper level to be sought and found. This is by no means a complete list of the many relational possibilities of family, and so *Jesus* sums it up in the phrase, "A man's enemies will be the members of his household." Well, what about the household of faith? Might these same dysfunctional ties exist there?

And the son said to him, "Father, I have sinned against heaven and in your sight; I am no longer worthy to be called your son." But the father said to his slaves, "Quickly bring out the best robe and put it on him, and put a ring on his hand and sandals on his feet; and bring the fattened calf, kill it, and let us eat and celebrate; for this son of mine was dead and has come to life again; he was lost and has been found." And they began to celebrate. (Luke 15:21-24)

Now his older son was in the field, and when he came and approached the house, he heard music and dancing. And he summoned one of the servants and began inquiring what these things could be. And he said to him, "Your brother has come, and your father has killed the fattened calf because he has received him back safe and sound." But he became angry and *was not willing* to go in; and his father came out and began pleading with him. But he answered and said to his father, "Look! For so many years I have been serving you and I have never neglected a command of yours; and yet you have never given me a young goat, so that I might celebrate with my friends, but when this son of yours came, who has devoured your wealth with prostitutes, you killed the fattened calf for him." And he said to him, "Son, you have always been with me, and all that is mine is yours." (Luke 15:25-31; italics mine)

The only place the elder brother had been alienated from the complete provision of his Father was in the hostility of his own carnal mind!

And although you were formerly alienated and hostile in mind, engaged in evil deeds, yet He has now reconciled you in His fleshly body through death, in order to present you before Him holy and *blameless* and *beyond* reproach *if indeed you continue in the faith firmly established and steadfast, and not moved away* from the hope of the gospel that you have heard, which was proclaimed in all creation under heaven, and of which I, Paul, was made a minister. *Now, I rejoice in my sufferings for your sake, and in my flesh I do my share on behalf of His body,* which is the church, in *filling up what is lacking in Christ's afflictions.* (Colossians 1:21-24; italics mine)

Many have the mistaken impression that those who press in to overcome are somehow involved in an egocentric pursuit. Here the use of the word *behalf* clearly states otherwise!

The benefit of any victory
you win
is not only won for yourself, but on
behalf of the body of Christ throughout eternity!

While you are pressing in for the victory and going through the purging of life's fiery trials, you need to be aware that you will be opposed by the very members of your own household. However,

it will lead to an opportunity for your testimony. "So make up your minds not to prepare beforehand to defend yourselves; for *I will give you utterance and wisdom which none of your opponents will be able to resist or refute.* But you will be betrayed even by parents and brothers and relatives and friends, and they will put some of you to death." (Luke 21:13-16; italics mine)

And they will put some of you to death.

But if you *die* in *love* for your betrayers, they can only bring your *victory*!

No man took *Jesus'* life! However, He did not hammer in His *own spikes*!

(By way of reminder, this is about the mind, the will, and the emotions.)

Allow me to spell this out for you. There are some in the household of faith that blindly preach a gospel of easy believe-ism that Jesus has done it all and that there is nothing more to be accomplished. This perfect little lie, along with a totally pain-free "I'm a Child of the King," name-it-and-claim-it, power-and-prosperity message is very seductive to the carnal mind. It's almost too good to be true, for now they can indulge the avarice of their prideful ego and to their hearts content while still feeling good about themselves. For after all, it's all now done in the name of *Jesus*!

You know what? God will give you the desires of your heart! He will abundantly bless your child of the flesh, your Christian Ishmael. Therefore, you will never know how you have been duped by your own carnality! That is until the day that He comes as a thief and takes it all away. But it's okay, I'm absolutely sure that a little "weeping and gnashing" will make it better.

If that sounds like a taunt, it is only because that is exactly what it is. The hour is late! If it takes the application of a little abrasive mud rubbed in the eyes of those who have been born blind — so be it! Nothing personal, I assure you! Now go wash and come again seeing!

Whenever this self-indulgent mind-set meets up with a believer who just doesn't seem to fit their understanding of how the kingdom works, they will consider him cursed and smitten of God! Clones of Job's counselors will come pouring out of the woodwork, accusing faultfinders convinced there is some hidden and horrendous sin lurking in the shadows.

They will wag their head in disgust and say things like, "I've never seen anyone who believed in the ultimate reconciliation of all that ever showed any fruit in their life." In their poverty, they will not see your riches; but in the compassion of your riches, you will clearly see their poverty. As they pin the instruments of your will to the cross of your victory, you will pray for those who despitefully use you! Stranger still, you will thank your Father for providing the means to do what you could never accomplish without their *aid*!

Truth is stranger than fiction! Many who read this book have already or will come into this very experience.

Knowing that we are eternally secure, Paul spoke of being "firmly established and steadfast, and not moved away from the hope of the gospel." He was speaking of taking full advantage of the hopeful provision of grace. Whereby we may, in this framework, work out the salvation of our mind, will, and emotions. Read carefully what the apostle Peter said concerning this:

> And *regard the patience of our Lord as salvation;* just as also our beloved brother Paul, according to the wisdom given him, wrote to you, as also in all his letters, speaking in them of these things, in which are some things hard to understand, which the untaught and unstable distort, as they do also the rest of the Scriptures, to their own destruction. [Yours also, if you are not wary!] (2 Peter 3:15-16)

> For My people have committed two evils: They have forsaken *Me, The fountain of living waters,* to hew for themselves cisterns, broken cisterns that can hold no water. (Jeremiah 2:13; italics mine)

And He who sits on the throne said, "Behold, I am making all things new." And He said, "Write, for these words are faithful and true." Then He said to me, "It is done. I am the Alpha and the Omega, the beginning and the end. *I will give to the one who thirsts from the spring of the water of life without cost.* He who overcomes will inherit these things, and I will be his God and he will be My son. But for the cowardly and unbelieving and abominable and murderers and immoral persons and sorcerers and idolaters and all liars, their part will be in the lake that burns with fire and brimstone, which is the second death." (Revelation 21:5-8; italics mine)

First, the King declares, "Behold, I am making all things new." Then even before He tells us how He is going to accomplish this amazing feat He gives us the assurance that it is an accomplished fact — one that can be trusted.

As the Alpha, He reminds us that every created thing came into being through Him (John 1:3). As the Omega, He is reminding us that all things shall find their ultimate consummation in Him (Ephesians 1:10). Next, He states that He "will give to the one who thirsts from the spring of the water of life without cost." There are no restrictions whatsoever placed upon anyone's access to this living water, and He states that He will freely give it to any that thirsts! Then He interjects something, which relates to "Behold, I am making all things new." He tells us, "He who overcomes will *inherit these things*, and I will be his God and he will be My son."

Finally, He tells us how everyone who has hewn for themselves a broken cistern and has not overcome the cowardly and unbelieving carnal nature is going to be made extremely thirsty by taking their part in the purifying lake that burns with fire and brimstone! (Remember our definitions.)

For all of history, man has tried to satiate his thirst from a broken cistern, "the wisdom of the world." This includes man's religious wisdom in an attempt to acquire power, glory, and honor. To accomplish this, he will lie, cheat, manipulate, and steal, with very little awareness of the true nature of his actions or their consequences. All because the one he has become most practiced at lying to is himself!

One must never be so audacious as to point this out!

Those who preach the "doctrine of hell" frequently use the parable of the rich man and Lazarus as a supposable proof text for their fallacy. However, only dishonestly will they ever refer to it as a parable, because they never look at it in a parabolic way. Rather doggedly, they insist it must be taken literally!

> Now there was a rich man, and he habitually dressed in purple and fine linen, joyously living in splendor every day. And a poor man named Lazarus was laid at his gate, covered with sores, and longing to be fed with the crumbs which were falling from the rich man's table; besides, even the dogs were coming and licking

133

his sores. Now the poor man died and was carried away by the angels to Abraham's bosom; and the rich man also died and was buried. In Hades he lifted up his eyes, being in torment, and saw Abraham far away and Lazarus in his bosom. And he cried out and said, "Father Abraham, have mercy on me, and send Lazarus so that he may dip the tip of his finger in water and cool off my tongue, for I am in agony in this flame." (Luke 16:19-24)

But Abraham said, "*Child, remember that during your life you received your good things, and likewise Lazarus bad things; but now he is being comforted here, and you are in agony*". "And besides all this, between us and you there is a great chasm fixed, so that those who wish to come over from here to you will not be able, and that none may cross over from there to us." And he said, "Then I beg you, father, that you send him to my father's house—for I have five brothers—in order that he may warn them, so that they will not also come to this place of torment." But Abraham said, "They have Moses and the Prophets; let them hear them." But he said, "No, father Abraham, but if someone goes to them from the dead, they will repent!" But he said to him, "If they do not listen to Moses and the Prophets, *they will not be persuaded even if someone rises from the dead*." (Luke 16:25-31; italics mine)

When we look at the parable literally, immediately a problem arises because *Jesus'* work on the cross then becomes meaningless. The rich man's fate in the "jaws of hell" is predicated upon how much he enjoyed his unfortunate blessing of wealth; something that the prosperity message overlooks. While Lazarus's apparent salvation is predicated upon how much he suffered in his poverty. At this rate, a man could buy his way into heaven by giving away his money. Hey, now there's an idea! Let's just divvy up the money evenly, that way, everyone can just go to "purgatory!" *Socialism! Yeah, that's the ticket!*

If the model that this parable portrays cannot be reconciled with the model understood as *salvation from eternal torment*, how may it legitimately be used as a *New Testament* proof text? Having to resort to smoke and mirrors and a little bit of booga booga (fear) should be a red flag that something might be just a little bit out of kilter!

Since we cannot make the parable fit *this particular model of salvation,* is there some aspect of the revealed word that it does portray? Undoubtedly, there are numerous interpretations that could be made, and most would likely result in valid, instructive, and profitable understanding. For as I said earlier, there are always many levels of understanding to be gleaned from the sayings of *Jesus.*

Therefore, regardless of whom the minor characters might represent, I would like us to look at the parable afresh and do so very objectively from a distance. We have two basic characters in this parable. One apparently rich in this world's goods and wisdom, and he spent his life thoroughly enjoying it. Then we have another person who, being poor in spirit, spent his life under very harsh circumstances, and was someone that no one in their "right mind" would envy. Next, we read that both of our intrepid characters have mutually suffered the wages of sin and have passed over to the other side. Here we see that some great cosmic equalizing principle of the universe seems to have balanced the books, and the roles are reversed.

In reading the parable, one particular passage seems to leap off the page.

> But Abraham said, "Child, remember that during your life you received your good things, and likewise Lazarus bad things; but now he is being comforted here, and you are in agony." (Luke 16:25)

I don't know about you, but I am immediately struck by the seemingly compassionate nonchalance that Jesus portrays Abraham's response to the "rich man." Almost to say in relative indifference, "Friend, do you not remember? The terms were always *buy now,* or *buy later*?"

> I advise you to buy from Me gold refined by fire so that you may become rich, and white garments so that you may clothe yourself, and that the shame of your nakedness will not be revealed; and eye salve to anoint your eyes so that you may see. (Revelation 3:18)

My child, clearly you chose to purchase later. And your problem is—

You say you are *thirsty* in the fire? You say you are in *torment*?

> Concordance reference—G928 torment
> basanizo
>
> Thayer definition:
> 1. To test (metals) by the touchstone, which is a black siliceous stone used to test the purity of gold or silver by the color of the streak produced on it by rubbing it with either metal
> 2. To question by applying torture
> 3. To torture
> 4. To vex with grievous pains (of body or mind), to torment
> 5. To be harassed, distressed
> 5a. Of those who at sea are struggling with a head wind
> Part of speech: verb

Well now, my wealthy friend, when the purity of the Master's gold is revealed against the touchstone of your torment, you, like Lazarus, shall be rich in the character of God! Then you will gratefully drink from our Father who is the Fountain of Living Waters. Incredibly, up until now, you may have never thirsted for His life-giving waters of refreshment, having become content in the *self-satisfied blindness* of religious carnality!

This forced baptism may very well be a violent eye-opener, but now, all may slake their thirst for the reality of union!

> Come, let us return to the Lord. For He has torn us, but He will heal us; He has wounded us, but He will bandage us. He will revive us after two days; He will raise us up on the third day that we may live before Him. (Hosea 6:1-2)

First by fire then by water, the understanding of all creation shall be purged of every ignorance, falsehood, and satanic-inspired deception. The fires of God will burn away anything that would threaten your perfect communion with the Father of lights.

And he shook off the beast into the fire, and felt no harm. (Acts 28:5)

Victory in Jesus

Having the mind's images, illusions, and reference points shattered has a tendency to leave one feeling just a little bit alone and out on a limb.

While at first, any unfamiliar territory may feel a bit uncomfortable this condition does pass. Soon you will take great comfort resting on the strong branch you presently find upholding you. Looking further out on this branch, you will come to notice it's made of a living understanding and is bearing fruit in your life.

Our aloneness or sense of isolation is actually an illusion itself, for we are never alone. God Himself has promised, "I will never desert you, nor will I ever forsake you." We have One who strengthens us. We need to realize that our Savior is not the least bit put off, nor is He surprised by the extent of man's carnality. It is the reason He went to the cross in the first place. He is fully aware of every aspect of how and why we stumble more so than we are in the blindness of it! In Him, we are able to rest and be strengthened for all the wonders that lie ahead. To whatever degree, we learn to rest in Him; He is able to keep us from stumbling. Allow the following words to minister grace to you:

> Therefore let us be diligent to enter that rest, so that no one will fall, through following the same example of disobedience. For the Word of God is living and active and sharper than any two-edged sword and piercing as far as the *division of soul and spirit*, of both joints and marrow, and able to judge the thoughts and intentions of the heart. And there is no creature hidden from His sight, but all things are open and laid bare to the eyes of Him with whom we have to do. *Therefore, since we have a great high priest who has passed through the heavens, Jesus the Son of God, let us hold fast our confession. For we do not have a high priest who cannot sympathize with our weaknesses*, but One who has been tempted in all things as we are, yet without sin. Therefore let us draw near with confidence to the throne of grace, so that we may receive mercy and find grace to help in time of need. (Hebrews 4:11-16; italics mine)

We do not need help with the world outside of us nearly as much as we need help with the world inside of us! His help speedily comes when we acknowledge our own weakness. Whenever we turn to rely upon His grace, His wisdom, and His intense interest in our affairs rather than the agenda of our own independent ideas, demands, and feelings, we do find rest for our souls. In this attitude of restful connection, we shall then find that we are empowered to overlook the world's offenses.

Only connected in this way with our Head, the Lord Jesus Christ, are we free to respond in love according to wisdom and *not react blindly* according to the dictates of our emotional programming? The more we practice, practice, practice *our connection* to love, the more balanced our emotional makeup will become.

For love shall soon be all in all.

"For I the LORD will speak, and whatever word I speak will be performed. It will no longer be delayed, for in your days, O rebellious house, I will speak the word and perform it," declares the Lord God. (Ezekiel 12:25)

Perfect peace, perfect poise, perfect power manifest to a hurting world, desperate to see the genuine article in God's children (sons). Amen and Amen.

The Conclusion of the Matter

He is coming to fill His temple. Even now, He is making preparations to fully cleanse His courts. This time, it will not be with whips and overturned tables wherewith He drives out the worldly ways of man. Rather it shall be with the all-consuming fire of His glory.

The gift of the Holy Spirit has been a rich blessing throughout the church age. We thank our Father wholeheartedly for this many-faceted blessing. Yet there is a further aspect of His awesome *gift*. Whereby, being *salted with fire* through God's glorious judgments, the *body of Christ* is made altogether pure: undefiled, without spot or wrinkle.

The fullness of Christ (Ephesians 4:13) will be revealed in His body when the legal arrangement of imputed righteousness is exchanged for a white robe. God's Holy Fire will ultimately reveal a righteousness that is actual and enduring.

> Until we all may come to the unity of the faith and of the full knowledge of the Son of God, to *a full-grown man, to the measure of the stature of the fullness of Christ.* (Ephesians 4:13; italics mine)

Our Lord said,

> I am come to send fire on the earth, and what will I, if it is already kindled? (Luke 12:49)

Again, our beloved brother Paul has instructed us:

> According to the grace of God which was given to me, like a wise master builder I laid a foundation, and another is building on it. But each man must be careful how he builds on it. For no man can lay a foundation other than the one which is laid, which is Jesus Christ. Now if any man builds on the foundation with gold, silver, precious stones, wood, hay, straw, each man's work will become evident; for the day will show it because it is to be revealed with fire, and the fire itself will test the quality of each man's work. If any man's work which he has built on it remains, he will receive a reward. If any man's work is burned up, he will suffer loss; but *he himself will be saved, yet so as through fire.* (1 Corinthians 3:10-15)

Brethren, once again, I implore you not to make a tragic mistake in thinking your work occurs on the outside of you. It may well be that it is reflected in the mirror of the world, but the actual work happens within!

We have also this witness from our favorite impetuous fisherman:

> But let not this one thing be hidden from you, beloved, that one day with the Lord is "as a thousand years, and a thousand years as one day." (Psalm 90:4)The Lord of the promise is not slow, as some deem slowness, but is long-suffering toward us, not having purposed any to perish but all to come to repentance. But the day of the Lord will come as a thief in the night in which the heavens will pass away with rushing sound; and having burned, the elements will be dissolved, and earth and the works in it will be burned up. Then all these being about to be dissolved, of what sort ought you to be in holy behavior and godliness, looking for and hastening the coming of the day of God through which the heavens, having been set afire, will be dissolved; and burning, the elements will melt. But according to His promise, we look for "new heavens and a new earth" in which righteousness dwells (Isaiah 65:17). Because of this, beloved, looking for these things, be diligent, spotless, and without blemish, to be found in peace with Him. (2 Peter 3:8-14; Literal Translation)

Even so, come, Lord Jesus. Dissolve our earthiness and melt these stony hearts that sit enthroned in the heavens of our soul.

My earnest prayer is that you have found the truths contained in this writing edifying to the body. For only in a love of "the Truth" and His brethren have I written to you.

In truth, you are clean through the word that has been spoken. Yet some may have found many concepts rather challenging to their currently accepted paradigms. I would encourage everyone to prove all things, including those things that heretofore may have never been questioned. Many may find, by reading this a second time, there are additional insights to be gleaned. This, because some things stated in the early chapters find support in understanding established later in the book.

I do not write to you as a scholar but as one whose heart has been captured by the Lord. Therefore, I have no wish to present this as the last word on anything. I am a firm believer that true wisdom shall only be found by the man who keeps his understanding upon a sacrificial altar, there to be tried in the undimmed light of God's counsel.

> And now, brothers, I commend you to God and to the Word of His grace, which is able to build up and to give you inheritance among all those being sanctified. (Acts 20:32; Literal Translation)

Go in peace, and may the Lord richly bless you in an ever-expanding awareness of the ways of His Kingdom.

John Van Tuyl
jvant2@cox.net

For those who enjoy poetry, the beautiful poem on the following pages expresses the true heart of this book.

The Blessing of a Storm

I did not know His love before,
The way I know it now.
I could not see my need for Him,
My pride would not allow.

I had it all, without a care,
The "self-sufficient" lie.
My path was smooth, my sea was still,
Not a cloud was in my sky.

*   *   *

I thought I knew His love for me,
I thought I'd seen His grace,
I thought I did not need to grow,
I thought I'd found my place.

But then the way grew rough and dark,
The storm clouds quickly rolled;
The waves began to rock my ship,
I found I had no hold.

*   *   *

The ship that I had built myself
Was made of foolish pride.
It fell apart and left me bare,
With nowhere else to hide.

I had no strength or faith to face
The trials that lay ahead,
And so I simply spoke His name
And bowed my weary head.

*   *   *

His loving arms enveloped me,
And then He helped me stand.
He said, "You still must face this storm,
But I will hold your hand."

So through the dark and lonely night
He guided me through pain.
I could not see the light of day
Or when I'd smile again.

*   *   *

Yet through the pain and endless tears,
My faith began to grow.
I could not see it at the time,
But my light began to glow.

I saw God's love in brand-new light,
His grace and mercy, too.
For only when all self was gone could
Jesus' love shines through.

*   *   *

It was not easy in the storm,
I sometimes wondered why.
At times I thought, "I can't go on."
I'd hurt, and doubt, and cry.

But Jesus never left my side,
He guided me each day.
Through pain and strife, and fire and flood,
He helped me all the way.

*   *   *

And now I see as ne'er before
How great His love can be,
How in my weakness He is strong,
How Jesus cares for me!

He worked it all out for my good,
Although the way was rough.
He only sent what I could bear,
And then He said, "Enough!"

*   *   *

He raised His hand and said, "Be still!"
He made the storm clouds cease.
He opened up the gates of joy
And flooded me with peace.

I saw His face now clearer still,
I felt His presence strong,
I found anew His faithfulness,
He never did me wrong.

*   *   *

And now I know more storms will come,
But only for my good,
For pain and tears have helped me grow
As nothing ever could.

I still have so much more to learn
As Jesus works in me;
If in the storm I'll love Him more,
That's where I want to be!

*   *   *

Wendy Greiner Lefko © 1996
Gratefully used by permission.